Cambridge English

Objective
Key

Teacher's Book
with Teacher's Resources
Audio CD/CD-ROM

Annette Capel   Wendy Sharp

Second Edition

CAMBRIDGE
UNIVERSITY PRESS

University Printing House, Cambridge CB2 8BS, United Kingdom

Cambridge University Press is part of the University of Cambridge.

It furthers the University's mission by disseminating knowledge in the pursuit of education, learning and research at the highest international levels of excellence.

www.cambridge.org
Information on this title: www.cambridge.org/9781107642041

First published 2005
3rd printing 2015

Printed in Italy by Rotolito Lombarda S.p.A.

A catalogue record for this publication is available from the British Library

ISBN 978-1-107-62724-6 Student's Book with Answers with CD-ROM
ISBN 978-1-107-66282-7 Student's Book without Answers with CD-ROM
ISBN 978-1-107-64204-1 Teacher's Book with Teacher's Resources Audio CD/CD-ROM
ISBN 978-1-107-69008-0 Class Audio CDs (2)
ISBN 978-1-107-64676-6 Workbook with Answers
ISBN 978-1-107-69921-2 Workbook without Answers
ISBN 978-1-107-66893-5 Student's Book Pack (Student's Book with Answers with CD-ROM and Class Audio CDs (2))
ISBN 978-1-107-60561-9 For Schools Practice Test Booklet with Answers with Audio CD
ISBN 978-1-107-69445-3 For Schools Pack (Student's Book and Practice Test Booklet without Answers with Audio CD)

Additional resources for this publication at www.cambridge.org/elt/objectivekey

Contents

Teacher's Resources Audio CD/CD-ROM

Practice tests with audio

10 Progress tests

Photocopiable activities

For Schools Pack Practice Test Booklet answers and recording scripts

Map of Objective Key Student's Book

TOPIC	EXAM SKILLS	GRAMMAR	VOCABULARY	PRONUNCIATION (P) AND SPELLING (S)
Unit 1 Friends 8–11 1.1 Friends for ever 1.2 Borrow this!	Paper 2 Listening: Part 1	Present simple: *be, have* Questions in the present tense	Personal possessions Adjectives	(P) The alphabet
Exam folder 1 12–13	Paper 2 Listening: Part 1 Short conversations			
Unit 2 Shopping 14–17 2.1 For sale 2.2 Shopping from home	Paper 1: Part 1 (Reading) Paper 2 Listening: Part 3	*How much ...?* *How many ...?* *some* and *any*	Shopping and shops	(P) /ɑː/ *car*, /eɪ/ *face*, /æ/ *apple* (S) Plurals
Exam folder 2 18–19	Paper 1 Reading and Writing: Part 1 (Reading) Notices			
Unit 3 Food and drink 20–23 3.1 Breakfast, lunch and dinner 3.2 Food at festivals	Paper 2 Listening: Part 5 Paper 1: Part 4 (Reading) Paper 1: Part 9 (Writing)	Present simple Telling the time Adverbs of frequency	Food and drink Celebrations Dates (day and month)	(S) Contractions (P) /ɪ/ *chicken*, /iː/ *cheese*
Writing folder 1 24–25	Paper 1 Reading and Writing: Part 6 (Writing) Spelling words			
Unit 4 The past 26–29 4.1 A real adventure 4.2 A mini-adventure	Paper 1: Part 4 (Reading) Paper 2 Listening: Part 5	Past simple Past simple: short answers Past simple + *ago*	Nationalities	(S) Regular verbs in the past simple (P) Regular past simple endings
Units 1–4 Revision 30–31				
Unit 5 Animals 32–35 5.1 Going to the zoo 5.2 An amazing animal	Paper 1: Part 6 (Writing) Paper 2 Listening: Part 3 Paper 1: Part 5 (Reading)	Lists with *and* Conjunctions *and, but, or, because*	Animals Collocations with *do, make, take* and *spend*	(P) List intonation (S) *their, there, they're*
Exam folder 3 36–37	Paper 1 Reading and Writing: Part 2 (Reading): Multiple choice Paper 1 Reading and Writing: Part 5 (Reading): Mulitple-choice cloze			
Unit 6 Leisure and hobbies 38–41 6.1 Theme park fun 6.2 Free time	Paper 3 Speaking: Part 2 Paper 3 Speaking: Part 1 Paper 2 Listening: Part 4 Paper 1: Part 9 (Writing) Paper 1: Part 2 (Reading)	Comparative and superlative adjectives Comparative adverbs	Leisure activities Descriptive adjectives and adverbs	(S) Comparative and superlative adjectives (P) /ə/ *camera*
Exam folder 4 42–43	Paper 2 Listening: Parts 4 and 5 Gap-fill			
Unit 7 Clothes 44–47 7.1 The latest fashion 7.2 Your clothes	Paper 1: Part 4 (Reading) Listening for information Paper 1: Part 3 (Reading)	Simple and continuous tenses	Clothes Adjectives to describe clothes	(S) *-ing* form (P) The last letters of the alphabet: w, x, y, z
Writing folder 2 48–49	Paper 1 Reading and Writing: Part 7 (Writing) Open cloze			
Unit 8 Entertainment 50–53 8.1 A great movie 8.2 Cool sounds	Paper 1: Part 5 (Reading) Paper 2 Listening: Part 1	Modal verbs 1: *must, have/had to, may, can, could*	Films, music	(P) Short questions (S) Mistakes with vowels
Units 5–8 Revision 54–55				

TOPIC	EXAM SKILLS	GRAMMAR	VOCABULARY	PRONUNCIATION (P) AND SPELLING (S)
Unit 9 Travel 56–59 9.1 Holiday plans 9.2 Looking into the future	Listening for information Paper 1: Part 3 (Reading) Paper 1: Part 7 (Writing)	The future with *going to* and *will*	Travel	(P) /h/ *hand* (S) Words ending in *-y*
Exam folder 5 60–61	Paper 3 Speaking: Parts 1 and 2			
Unit 10 Places and buildings 62–65 10.1 Inside the home 10.2 Famous buildings	Paper 2 Listening: Part 2 Paper 1: Part 2 (Reading)	The passive – present and past simple	Furniture, rooms Colours, materials Opposites	(S) Words ending in *-f* and *-fe* (P) Dates (years)
Exam folder 6 66–67	Paper 1 Reading and Writing: Part 4 (Reading) Right, Wrong, Doesn't say			
Unit 11 Sport 68–71 11.1 Living for sport 11.2 Keeping fit	Paper 1: Part 4 (Reading) Paper 2 Listening: Part 5 Paper 1: Part 6 (Writing)	Word order in questions Verbs in the *-ing* form	Sport and sports equipment Fitness	(P) /b/ *basketball*, /v/ *volleyball* (S) *gu-, qu-*
Writing folder 3 72–73	Paper 1 Reading and Writing: Part 9 (Writing) Short message			
Unit 12 The family 74–77 12.1 Family tree 12.2 Large and small	Paper 2 Listening: Part 3 Paper 1: Part 4 (Reading)	Possessive adjectives and pronouns Subject, object and reflexive pronouns *everything, something, anything,* etc.	People in a family	(P) /aʊ/ *cow*, /ɔː/ *draw* (S) Words ending in *-le*
Units 9–12 Revision 78–79				
Unit 13 The weather 80–83 13.1 Sun, rain or snow? 13.2 Weather problems	Paper 2 Listening: Part 2 Paper 1: Part 5 (Reading)	*(not) as ... as* *enough* and *too*	Weather	(P) Unstressed words with /ə/ (S) *to, too* and *two*
Exam folder 7 84–85	Paper 2 Listening: Part 2 Multiple matching			
Unit 14 Books and studying 86–89 14.1 Something good to read 14.2 Learn something new!	Paper 1: Part 4 (Reading) Paper 2 Listening: Part 4 Paper 1: Part 3 (Reading)	Position of adjectives *I prefer / I'd like*	Books School subjects, education	(P) Silent consonants (S) Words which are often confused
Exam folder 8 90–91	Paper 1 Reading and Writing: Part 3 (Reading) Multiple choice			
Unit 15 The world of work 92–95 15.1 Working hours 15.2 Part-time jobs	Paper 1: Part 4 (Reading) Paper 2 Listening: Part 3	Present perfect *just* and *yet*	Work, jobs	(S) Words ending in *-er* and *-or* (P) /ð/ *clothes*, /θ/ *thirsty*
Writing folder 4 96–97	Paper 1 Reading and Writing: Part 8 (Writing) Information transfer			
Unit 16 Transport 98–101 16.1 Journeys 16.2 A day out	Paper 3 Speaking: Part 2 Paper 2 Listening: Part 1	Modal verbs 2: *must, mustn't, don't have to, should, need to, needn't*	Transport Collocations with transport Free-time activities Directions	(P) Weak and strong forms (S) *i* or *e*?
Units 13–16 Revision 102–103				
Unit 17 Science and technology 104–107 17.1 Totally Techno 17.2 New ideas	Paper 1: Part 5 (Reading) Paper 2 Listening: Part 3	Infinitive of purpose The infinitive with and without *to*	Technology Collocations with *get, give, have, make, see, watch*	(P) Contractions (S) Correcting mistakes

TOPIC	EXAM SKILLS	GRAMMAR	VOCABULARY	PRONUNCIATION (P) AND SPELLING (S)
Exam folder 9 108–109	Paper 2 Listening: Part 3 Multiple choice			
Unit 18 Health and well-being 110–113 18.1 Keeping well! 18.2 A long and happy life	Paper 1: Part 6 (Writing) Paper 1: Parts 3 and 4 (Reading) Paper 2 Listening: Part 5 Paper 1: Part 9 (Writing)	Word order of time phrases First conditional	Parts of the body Health	(P) Linking sounds (S) Words which don't double their last letter
Exam folder 10 114–117	Paper 1 Reading and Writing: Part 4 (Reading) Multiple choice			
Unit 19 Language and communication 118–121 19.1 Let's communicate! 19.2 Different languages	Paper 2 Listening: Part 2 Paper 1: Part 7 (Writing) Paper 1: Part 5 (Reading)	Prepositions of place Prepositions of time	Communicating Countries, languages, nationalities	(P) Word stress (S) Spellings of the sound /iː/
Writing folder 5 122–123	Paper 1 Reading and Writing: Part 9 (Writing) Short message			
Unit 20 People 124–127 20.1 Famous people 20.2 Lucky people	Paper 1: Part 4 (Reading) Paper 2 Listening: Part 4 Paper 3 Speaking: Part 2 Paper 1: Part 6 (Writing) Paper 1: Part 2 (Reading)	Review of tenses	Describing people	(P) Sentence stress (S) *ck* or *k*?
Units 17–20 Revision 128–129				
Extra material 130–135				
Grammar folder 136–148				
Vocabulary folder 149–153				
Practice for Key Writing Part 6 154–158				
List of irregular verbs 159				

Content of Cambridge English: Key

The Cambridge English: Key (and Key for Schools) examination is at A2 level of the Common European Framework. There are three papers – Paper 1 Reading and Writing, Paper 2 Listening and Paper 3 Speaking.

There are five grades: Pass with Merit (about 85% of the total marks) and Pass (about 70% of the total marks) are passing grades at A2 level. An additional grade of Pass with Distinction records a pass at B1 level. A Narrow Fail (about 5% below the pass mark) records A1 level achievement. For this and the Fail grade, the results slip will show the papers which had particularly low marks.

Paper 1 Reading and Writing 1 hour 10 minutes   (50% of the total marks)

There are nine parts in this paper and they are always in the same order. Parts 1–5 test a range of reading skills and Parts 6–9 test basic writing skills. You write all your answers on the answer sheet.

Part	Task type	Number of questions	Task format	Objective Exam folder
Reading Part 1	Matching	5	You match five sentences to eight notices.	EF 2
Reading Part 2	Multiple choice (A, B or C)	5	You choose the right words to complete five sentences.	EF 3
Reading Part 3	Multiple choice (A, B or C) AND Matching	5	You choose the right answer to complete short conversational exchanges.	EF 8
Reading Part 4	Right / Wrong / Doesn't say OR Multiple choice (A, B or C)	7 7	You answer seven questions on a text. OR You read a text and choose the right answer to seven questions.	EF 6 EF 10
Reading Part 5	Multiple choice (A, B or C)	8	You choose the right words to complete eight spaces in a short text.	EF 3
Writing Part 6	Word completion	5	You decide which words go with five definitions and spell them correctly.	WF 1
Writing Part 7	Open cloze	10	You fill ten spaces in a text such as a postcard with single words, spelled correctly.	WF 2
Writing Part 8	Information transfer	5	You complete a set of notes or a form with information from one or two texts.	WF 4
Writing Part 9	Short message	1	You write a short message, such as a note, an email or a postcard (25–35 words), which includes three pieces of information.	WF 3, WF 5

Paper 2 Listening about 30 minutes (including 8 minutes to transfer answers) (25% of the total marks)

There are five parts in this paper and they are always in the same order. You hear each recording twice.
You write your answers on the answer sheet at the end of the test.

Part	Task type	Number of Questions	Task format	Objective Exam folder
Listening Part 1	Multiple choice (A, B or C)	5	You answer five questions by choosing the correct picture, word or number. There are two speakers in each short conversation.	EF 1
Listening Part 2	Matching	5	You match five questions with eight possible answers. There are two speakers.	EF 7
Listening Part 3	Multiple choice (A, B or C)	5	You answer five questions about a conversation between two speakers.	EF 9
Listening Part 4	Gap-fill	5	You complete five spaces in a set of notes. There are two speakers.	EF 4
Listening Part 5	Gap-fill	5	You complete five spaces in a set of notes. There is one speaker.	EF 4

Paper 3 Speaking 8–10 minutes for a pair of students (25% of the total marks)

There are two parts to the test and they are always in the same order. There are two candidates and two examiners. Only one of the examiners asks the questions.

Part	Task type	Time	Task format	Objective Exam folder
Speaking Part 1	The examiner asks both candidates some questions.	5–6 minutes	You must give information about yourself.	EF 5
Speaking Part 2	The candidates talk together to find out information.	3–4 minutes	You are given some material to help you ask and answer questions.	EF 5

CONTENT OF CAMBRIDGE ENGLISH: KEY

Introduction to the Second Edition

What is new about this second edition?

The second edition of *Objective Key* has been informed by the English Vocabulary Profile (see below). In addition, following consultation with users of the course worldwide, the material has been updated where necessary and extended, with additional practice for the *Cambridge English: Key* and *Key for Schools* exams now available.

Student's Book with CD-ROM

The unit topics are unchanged but some of the texts are new, together with new illustrations and photos, additional exercises and new audio recordings. Two new features in the units – Key speaking and Key words – highlight useful language for students, and the Key words icon also takes them to the enlarged Vocabulary Folder. There is also a new section of vocabulary practice for Writing Part 6 of the exam, which exploits the contents of the Vocabulary Folder. The Student's Book includes a new CD-ROM. The CD-ROM provides many interactive activities, including grammar, vocabulary, listening and reading and writing. Games make practising the language fun. All the extra activities are linked to topics in the Student's Book.

Workbook

This has been revised and offers further practice in grammar, vocabulary and exam skills.

Teacher's Book with Teacher's Resources Audio CD/CD-ROM

The Teacher's Resources Audio CD/ CD-ROM that accompanies the Teacher's Book provides a selection of photocopiable resources. There are 10 progress tests, covering important grammar, vocabulary and spelling, for each pair of units. The spelling section has been informed by the most common errors made by exam candidates, taken from the *Key* and *Key for Schools* data in the Cambridge Learner Corpus. In addition, there are two complete practice tests with audio on the Audio CD/ CD-ROM. You will also find the Answer key and recording scripts for the *For Schools Pack* Practice Test Booklet here.

Website

The second edition also has a dedicated website: www. cambridge.org/elt/objectivekey. The website contains further grammar and vocabulary practice for students.

What is English Profile?

English Profile is a long-term research programme that is seeking to describe what learners know and can do in English at each level of the Common European Framework of Reference (CEFR). The CEFR is 'language-neutral', as it is designed to work for all languages. A number of English Profile projects, initially targeting grammar, functions and vocabulary, will illustrate in detail what the CEFR means for English.

A key feature of English Profile is its empirical approach. Its researchers make extensive use of various corpora of language data, including the largest analysed corpus of learner data in the world: the Cambridge Learner Corpus. This contains learner writing at all levels of the CEFR from more than 200 countries.

What is the English Vocabulary Profile?

The English Vocabulary Profile is an interactive web resource that provides detailed information on the words, phrases, phrasal verbs and idioms that are known by learners at each level of the CEFR. There are approximately 1500 headword entries up to A2 level and around 7000 in the complete A1–C2 resource. Each entry presents individual meanings of a word in CEFR order, to suggest learning priorities. For example, the entry for the word *stage* has the meaning THEATRE – the raised area in a theatre where actors perform – at A2 and PART – a period of development, or a particular time in a process – at B2.

The English Vocabulary Profile lists many phrases within its entries, so the entry for the noun *way* includes *by the way* at A2 and useful phrases such as *one way or another, make your way* and *in a way* at B2. Phrasal verbs are included at the end of an entry, and it is possible to search for words, phrases, phrasal verbs and idioms as separate categories by level.

How has this new edition of *Objective Key* been informed by the English Vocabulary Profile?

Having access to the online resource during the writing of the second edition has enabled us to check the level of all the vocabulary used in the first edition, as well as providing us with additional level-appropriate words and phrases for individual units. Within the Advanced search facility of the English Vocabulary Profile, it is possible to use various filters to narrow down the search results – for example, to obtain all A2 adjectives for a certain topic or a list of useful phrases that are likely to be known at this level. This has added to the breadth and reliability of the course content.

How to get involved in English Profile

The English Profile Programme is developing a new corpus of learner English – the Cambridge English Profile Corpus – which will include both spoken and written data. You and your students can get involved! Joining the data contributor network is straightforward and has many benefits. Visit the English Profile website to find out more at www.englishprofile.org, where you will also be able to sign up to the English Vocabulary Profile itself.

1 Friends

Preparation

Make a copy of the recording script on the Teacher's CD-ROM (Photocopiable activities, page 2) for each student. This will be used in 1.1.

1.1 Friends for ever
SB pages 8–9

1   The twelve reasons contain examples of the present simple of the verbs *be* and *have*, which will be revised in the Grammar extra that follows exercise 1. Suggest that students read the sentences in pairs or threes and say which are true for them. They can decide together which is the most important reason. Elicit their views. Then give students two minutes to write three more reasons in their groups. Elicit their sentences and write some on the board.

Extension activity

If students enjoy thinking of further reasons why friends are great, suggest they make a large poster for the classroom wall, displaying their own ideas. They could include pictures from magazines to illustrate their reasons, as on the Student's Book page.

Grammar extra

2   Ask students to complete the verb boxes, looking back at the sentences in exercise 1 if necessary. Point out that the full negative form *I am not, I have not*, etc. is also correct, although this is not practised here.

Answers

The verb *be*	The verb *have*
I am, I'm, I'm not	I have, I've, I haven't
you are, you're, you aren't	you have, you've, you haven't
he/she/it is, he's, she isn't	he/she/it has, he's, she hasn't
we are, we're, we aren't	we have, we've, we haven't
they are, they're, they aren't	they have, they've, they haven't

Pronunciation

3   **Key Speaking Part 1**

1 02 Students will have to spell something, such as their surname, in the first part of the Speaking test. They are also tested on their ability to write down words that are spelled out in Parts 4 and 5 of the Listening test, for example a name, part of an address, etc. This exercise checks whether students are familiar with the whole alphabet – all the letters apart from Q and X are covered in the six names.

Practise spelling in this way regularly during the course.

Before playing the recording, run through the whole alphabet with the class, eliciting a letter from each student in turn.

After the recording, point out the use of *double B* in question 5 and *double O* in question 6. Two of the same letters or numbers together will be said like this in the *Key* Listening test.

Recording script and answers
1   NOVAK DJOKOVIC
2   PENELOPE CRUZ
3   BART SIMPSON
4   TAYE TAIWO
5   THE HOBBIT
6   THE FOO FIGHTERS

Listening

4   **Key Listening Part 1**

1 03 This listening activity includes further spelling practice and introduces students to short conversations, with an emphasis on questions and answers. The recordings here are slightly slower and simpler than those candidates will hear in the exam, to build students' confidence.

Ask students to listen and complete the information. If they are particularly weak in listening, play the recording twice and suggest they don't write anything down the first time they listen.

Answers
1   13; play football
2   Raquel; every day
3   Vicky; her sister; 13
4   Lucky / his dog; to the river

Recording script

1

Maria: OK, Matt, let's start with you. What's your best friend called?

Matt: Er, Jonny, and he's thirteen, the same as me.

Maria: Right, and what do you do together, you know, in your free time?

Matt: That's easy to answer. We play football, as much as possible. We're in the same team, you see.

2

Maria: And Elena, what can you tell me about your best friend?

Elena: Well, her name's Raquel. Shall I spell that? It's R-A-Q-U-E-L.

Maria: Uh huh. And when do you get together? Like, just at weekends?

Elena: Oh no, we're best friends, Maria! I see Raquel every day … in school Monday to Friday … and then we go out at weekends.

3

Maria: Kelly-Anne, I know your best friend is Vicky. Do you spell that V-I-C-K-Y?

Kelly-Anne: That's right.

Maria: And do you see her every day?

Kelly-Anne: Yes, because Vicky's my sister.

Maria: Mmm, that's a really special friend. So how old are you, Kelly-Anne?

Kelly-Anne: It's my birthday next week. I'll be fourteen … so I'm thirteen now.

4

Maria: Hi, Tom! Come here so I can ask you some questions. Who's your best friend?

Tom: My best friend … huh, that's difficult. I mean, I've got lots of friends, but a best friend? I'd say it's Lucky, my dog. You spell that L-U-C-K-Y.

Maria: Ah, that's sweet. So where do you go with Lucky? Do you take him for walks?

Tom: Of course, every day! We go to the river. Lucky likes the water!

Maria: Hope he can swim. OK, thanks, all you guys. See you.

All: Bye!

Photocopiable recording script activity ◎

Hand out copies of the recording script from the Teacher's Audio CD/CD-ROM (Photocopiable activities page 2), asking students to fill in the missing words as they listen to the recording again.

Answers
1 team
2 Monday to Friday
3 special
4 dog

---

5 **1 04** Students will hear Maria asking questions and should write their answers as they listen. Remind them to write short answers, as they won't have time to write much.

Pauses between questions have been included on the recording but, if necessary, stop the recording between questions, to give students longer to write their answers.

6 Encourage students to use some of the language given, as this will make their questions and answers sound more natural. The *Key speaking* and *Key words* boxes feature useful words and phrases for the exam, informed by the English Vocabulary Profile.

English Profile
The second edition of *Objective Key* has been informed by the English Vocabulary Profile, a detailed description of the words and phrases known by learners at each level of the Common European Framework of Reference (CEFR). For more information, visit www.englishprofile.org

1.2 Borrow this!
SB pages 10–11

1 Check that students understand the two verbs *borrow* and *lend*, explaining the difference if necessary. Then give students two or three minutes to discuss the questions. Elicit students' answers and ask whether they ever have any problems when lending things to friends. Check they understand the meaning of *give back*.

2 Ask students to read the photo story in pairs to find out why Sam is angry at the beginning but not at the end. The story includes examples of different question forms, which will be looked at in the Grammar section.

Answers
Sam is angry at the beginning because Gary's got his DVDs.
Sam isn't angry at the end because he hears that Gary is having problems at school.

Grammar

3 Ask students to read through the story again and find one *Yes/No* question and one *Wh-* question.

Answers
Yes/No questions:
Do you know about Gary's problems?
Is he OK?
Has Gary got your *Avatar* DVD?
Are you free tonight, Sam?
Can you text him about my DVDs?

Wh- questions:
When do you want them back?
What can we see?

The suggestion forms *Why don't ...* and *How about ...* are included because of the problems *Key* students have in using them accurately. Draw students' attention to the fact that *How about ...* is followed by a verb in the *-ing* form.

Ask students to read the grammar rules on their own, adding their own example questions. Elicit these.

4 These sentences are taken from the *Key* section of the *Cambridge Learner Corpus*. This is a large collection of past exam candidates' scripts, which has been compiled jointly by the University of Cambridge ESOL Examinations and Cambridge University Press. The authors have consulted the *Learner Corpus* extensively in the development of *Objective Key*.

Ask students to correct the questions as necessary and compare their answers with another student.

Answers
1 When *do* you want to come here?
2 Where *are you* now?
3 How about *meeting* me at 7 o'clock?
4 (correct)
5 Why *do* you think it is interesting?
6 (correct)
7 Who *does he* like?

5 This exercise gives students further practice in forming *Wh-* questions. Go round listening to each pair, correcting their word order if necessary.

Vocabulary

6 The adjectives have all appeared in Unit 1. If time is short, this exercise can be set for homework.

Answers
1 lucky
2 sick
3 free
4 horrible
5 pleased
6 worried
7 amazing
8 popular
Three more adjectives are: different (4), angry (6), boring (8).
The extra adjective in the box is *true*.

Activity

Ask students to work with a partner and turn to the questionnaire on page 130 of the Student's Book. Tell them to take turns to ask questions and complete a questionnaire about their partner. Elicit information at the end if there is time.

Exam folder 1

SB pages 12–13

Listening Part 1
Short conversations

Ask students to read the information about this part of the Listening paper. Explain that they will have eight minutes at the end of the test to transfer all their answers to the answer sheet.

Tell students to look at the example of the answer sheet for Part 1 and make sure they know how to fill it in correctly. Marks are often lost because candidates complete the answer sheet incorrectly.

It is useful for students to work with recording scripts, especially at the beginning of a course, as this builds their confidence and allows them to understand how each part of the Listening test is structured.

Ask students to follow the procedure as they read the example recording script. Elicit the correct answer (A).

1 05 Refer students to the Exam advice box and give them a couple of minutes to read and discuss it. Then ask them to follow the same procedure as they do the exam task.

Answers
1 C 2 A 3 A 4 B 5 C

Recording script
You will hear five short conversations.
You will hear each conversation twice.
There is one question for each conversation.
For questions 1–5, put a tick under the right answer.

1 *What is the man buying for his lunch?*
Woman: Can I help you, Mr Stoker? Some soup, as usual?
Man: Not today, thanks. But I'd like something hot – a slice of that pizza, please.
Woman: OK. Anything else?
Man: Just some egg sandwiches for Sally. I'm taking them back to her desk. She's very busy.
Now listen again.
(The recording is repeated.)
2 *When is Maria's party?*
Woman: David, you know it's my birthday on Friday. Are you free to come to my party?

Man: Oh dear, Maria, I'm in London that day. Can I take you to a restaurant on Saturday instead?
Woman: That's a great idea, and you can still come to my party because it's on Wednesday. It starts at eight thirty.
Man: Great!
Now listen again.
(The recording is repeated.)

3 *Which postcard does the woman choose?*
Man: Are you getting a postcard for your sister? Here's a beautiful one of the lake.
Woman: But we didn't go there. I only send cards of places I know. This one of the city at night looks good.
Man: I agree, but your sister doesn't like cities!
Woman: You're right, I'll get her the forest one. We went there two days ago, remember?
Now listen again.
(The recording is repeated.)

4 *How much does the woman pay for the DVD?*
Woman: I want to buy an *Avatar* film on DVD. Have you got any under ten pounds?
Man: I'm sorry, no. The new one's nineteen pounds fifty, and that's not a bad price. How about buying the one before that? That's only ten pounds fifty.
Woman: OK, I'll take that one. Here's twenty pounds.
Man: Thank you, and that's nine pounds fifty back. Enjoy it.
Now listen again.
(The recording is repeated.)

5 *What did the girl leave at Ben's flat?*
Girl: Hello, Ben. Thanks for the coffee this afternoon. I think the lights for my bike are on your kitchen table. I put them down there when you gave me my jacket, remember?
Ben: They are. I found them next to my books just now.
Girl: Sorry. Can you bring them to college tomorrow, please?
Ben: No problem.
Now listen again.
(The recording is repeated.)

2 Shopping

2.1 For sale	
Vocabulary	Shops and items you buy in them
Grammar extra	Questions with countable and uncountable nouns
Exam skills	Reading Part 1: Notices
Pronunciation	Vowel sounds /ɑː/, /eɪ/ and /æ/

2.2 Shopping from home	
Exam skills	Listening (and Reading) Part 3: Multiple choice
Grammar	*some* and *any*
Spelling	Plurals

Preparation

For the Extension activity in Lesson 2.2 make copies of the *Number Bingo* cards on the Teacher's Audio CD/CD-ROM (Photocopiable activities, page 3), enough for each student to have one card, and cut them up.

2.1 For sale

SB pages 14–15

Vocabulary

1 Ask students to spend two minutes on this warm-up activity. Elicit which goods are sold in each place.

Answers
1 *market*: carrots, fish, tomatoes, cheese, apples, potatoes
2 *bookshop*: books, DVD, map, magazine, birthday card
3 *chemist*: (cough) medicine, shampoo, soap
4 *department store*: belt, camera, sunglasses, sweater, umbrella, wallet
5 *sports shop*: tennis racket, tennis balls, trainers, football

2 Encourage students to write down new vocabulary in meaningful lists. If they don't already keep a vocabulary notebook, suggest this would be useful. They could organise it according to the unit topics in the Student's Book, which represent the topics in the *Key* exam.

3 Elicit answers to these questions. Then refer students to the Grammar extra box to consolidate the difference between *How much* and *How many*.

4 Tell students to ask and answer in pairs.

Reading

5 *Key* Reading Part 1

Ask students to look through the notices quickly without reading them and suggest where each notice might be found.

Answers
A on (wool or silk) clothing, e.g. a sweater or dress
B in a supermarket car park
C on a shoe box
D on a menu / at a restaurant
E on a market stall / in a shop
F on a poster/wall/door
G in a shop window
H in a newspaper

6 This is a training activity for the Reading Part 1 matching task, which also revises alphabet use. Because part of each text is missing, students must read the notices very carefully and think about their content. Give students five minutes to write down the missing letters. Then elicit answers, asking students to spell out the letters. Write the full words on the board.

Answers
A HA B PA C MA D PA; SA E CA F SA; TI
G CA; SA H AD; GA; ON; PH

7

Answers
1 G 2 D 3 H 4 B 5 A

Pronunciation

8 1 06 The vowel sounds /ɑː/ as in car, /eɪ/ as in *face* and /æ/ as in *apple* are sometimes confused. The sounds are shown here with pictures to help students remember them. Students have already seen most of the words, but check understanding before they listen.

Ask students to listen and repeat each word, and underline the relevant sound each time.

Answers
/ɑː/ c<u>ar</u> super<u>mar</u>ket <u>ar</u>tist dep<u>ar</u>tment store
/eɪ/ f<u>a</u>ce s<u>a</u>le Pl<u>a</u>yStation em<u>ai</u>l
/æ/ <u>a</u>pple m<u>a</u>p c<u>a</u>rrot <u>a</u>dvert

9 Ask students to look back at the notices in exercise 6 to find more words with the sounds /ɑː/, /eɪ/ and /æ/. Some of the words are those with missing letters.

Answers
/ɑː/ half, parking
/eɪ/ made, games, eight (8)
/æ/ hand, cameras, pasta, salad, and(&), Saturday

2.2 Shopping from home
SB pages 16–17

1 Give students two minutes to discuss the different ways of shopping: ordering from a catalogue and buying on the Internet. Then elicit answers. Suggest reasons for and against shopping from home if necessary.

(*For* – it saves time and can be cheaper; *against* – it is less fun and you can't see the goods you're buying.)

Listening

2 **Key** Listening Part 3 and Reading Part 3

This training activity supports students by presenting most of the recording script on the page and allowing them to predict what they will hear. The answers are confined to numbers and prices. Note that the printed conversation takes the form of a Reading Part 3 task, where candidates have to match responses.

Ask students to tell you what the conversation is about.

Answer
Ordering goods from a sportswear catalogue

3 **1 07** Play the recording and ask students to listen and fill in the missing numbers.

Answers
1 14 2 (£)26.40 3 57 4 (£)18.95 5 38

Recording script
Kevin: Good morning. Sportswear, Kevin speaking. How can I help you?
Sally: Hi. I've got your catalogue here, but I can't find the price list. Can you give me some prices?
Kevin: Of course. Please tell me the page number you're looking at.
Sally: OK. The first thing is on page 14 and it's the football shirt, the blue and red one.

Kevin: OK, the small and medium sizes are £22.65 and large and extra-large are £26.40.
Sally: Right. I'd like to order one, please, size small.
Kevin: Fine. Have you got any more things to order?
Sally: Yes, I'd like some trainers. They're on page 57. How much are the black and purple ones at the top of the page?
Kevin: Well, they *were* £49.50 but they're in the sale now, so they're only £18.95. But we don't have any left in small sizes. What shoe size are you?
Sally: I'm a 38.
Kevin: Let me check. Wow, you're lucky! We've got one pair in that size.
Sally: Great. Well, that's all I need. My name and address is …

Extension activity
If students seem weak on their numbers, play *Number Bingo* with them. To do this, you will need to prepare a set of cards from the photocopiable material on the Teacher's Audio CD/CD-ROM. The activity covers the numbers 1 to 50 and there are eight different cards. (Make sure students sitting together do not get the same card.) Hand out one card to each student or, in large classes, ask students to work in pairs. Students should tick any numbers on their cards that they hear you say. The first student to complete a card shouts 'Bingo'. Ask that student to read out the numbers ticked, as a check.

Grammar

4 Ask students to read sentences 1–5 and complete rules a–e. Elicit answers to this matching task.

Answers
a some – sentence 2   b any – sentence 4
c some – sentence 1   d some – sentence 5
e any – sentence 3

5 Ask students to complete sentences 1–9 on their own and then compare answers.

Answers
2 some 3 any 4 some 5 some 6 some 7 any
8 some 9 any; some

6   Give students time to read the information carefully. Then ask them to work out the plural forms of the words in the exercise by following the rules in a–f and say which group (a–f) the words belong to.

Answers
baby – babies   group **e**
coach – coaches   group **b**
dress – dresses   group **b**
monkey – monkeys   group **d**
potato – potatoes   group **c**
tooth – teeth   group **f**
window – windows   group **a**

Explain that the activity practises plural spellings. Students can work in pairs.

Answers
1 map – maps   2 camera – cameras   3 bus – buses
4 dress – dresses   5 book – books   6 bicycle – bicycles
7 fly – flies   8 rice – rice   9 box, boxes
10 banana – bananas   11 arm – arms   12 glass – glasses
13 tomato – tomatoes   14 potato – potatoes
15 lion – lions

The four words say PASS KEY EXAM SOON.

Exam folder 2

SB pages 18–19

Reading Part 1 Notices

Ask students to read the information about this part of the Reading and Writing paper.

1   This task shows students some of the key areas of language that are tested in this part of the Reading paper. Elicit further examples for each one.

Possible answers
1 you should   2 bigger   3 Keep quiet
4 at 6.30; on Sunday   5 in the field

2   Suggest students work in pairs to find examples of the language areas above in the exam task questions on page 19.

Answers
1   (modal verbs)
    Question 4: you can
    Question 5: you may
2   (comparison)
    Question 1: later
    Question 2: cheaper
    Question 3: lower
    Question 5: younger
    Notice H: longer
3   (imperatives)
    Example o: Do not leave
    Notice A: Buy
    Notice D: Please put
    Notice G: Spend

4   (prepositions with times/ days)
    Notice C: from 7 pm
    Notice E: until then (next Tuesday)
5   (prepositions with places)
    Example o: on the floor
    Notice A: at machine
    Notice D: above your seat

Refer students to the Exam advice box and make sure they understand the advice given. Ask them to follow this procedure as they do the exam task. Also draw their attention to the example of the candidate answer sheet and make sure they know how to fill it in correctly.

Part 1

Allow students a maximum of six minutes to complete the task.

Answers
1 H   2 B   3 E   4 A   5 F

3 Food and drink

Preparation

Make one copy of the *Britain and …* fact sheet on the Teacher's Audio CD/CD-ROM (Photocopiable activities, page 4) for each student for the Extension activity in 3.2.

3.1 Breakfast, lunch and dinner

SB pages 20–21

Vocabulary

1 Writing Part 6 tests the spelling of lexical items. In the exam, there are five dictionary-type definitions and students need to identify and then spell the item. In this unit there is some preliminary work for this part of the exam.

Ask students to work in pairs. They should talk about the photos and tell each other what they can see.

Ask individual students to come up and write on the board one item of food or drink they can see in the photos. The class should say if the student has spelled the word correctly.

Answers
1 potatoes, rice, pasta, bread
2 pizza, sandwich, burger, soup
3 tomatoes, carrots, onions, salad
4 apples, grapes, bananas, oranges
5 lemonade, orange juice, mineral water, coffee
6 steak, chicken, fish, cheese
7 ice cream, cake, biscuits, chocolate

Give the class time to write down the words in their vocabulary books.

Students should then close their vocabulary books and do the word puzzle. This can be done in class or for homework.

Answers
1 grapes 2 apple 3 fish 4 tomato 5 chocolate
6 burger 7 orange 8 salad 9 sandwich 10 steak

The word in the yellow squares is *restaurant*.

Ask students to look at the photos of the different food groups. Invite them to say why the foods are in those particular groups, i.e. what the foods in each group have in common.

Suggested answers
photo 1: carbohydrates / filling foods
photo 2: lunch items / snacks / fast food
photo 3: vegetables
photo 4: fruit
photo 5: drinks
photo 6: food containing protein (meat, fish, cheese)
photo 7: dessert/sweet/sugary food

Extension activity

To extend vocabulary, ask: *In the photos, what is the item of food or drink in/on?*
Answers
fruit – in a bowl sandwich – on a plate
burger – in a bun soup – in a bowl biscuits – on a plate
potatoes – in a supermarket basket
lemonade – in a bottle orange juice – in a carton
coffee – in a cup

Put the names of other containers (*box, can/tin, jug, glass, packet, jar*) on the board and ask the class, either in pairs or groups, to write down what they think they would find in the containers. This can be done as a game (the first pair or group to finish, with correct answers, are the winners), for homework or just as a vocabulary extension in class.

Pronunciation

2 **1 08** The focus is on the sounds /ɪ/ as in *chicken* and /iː/ as in *cheese*. Draw students' attention to the pictures. Ask students to repeat each word after the recording.

Then ask them to form pairs. Each pair should draw two columns on a piece of paper. They should decide which column each word goes in.

1 09 Play the next track when they have finished so they can check their answers.

Answers	
group 1 /ɪ/ chicken	*group 2 /iː/ cheese*
bin	beans
biscuit	eat
chips	feel
dinner	leave
fill	meal
fish	meat
live	seat
sit	tea

You could do some spelling practice by asking students to write down the words you say. Choose five words from each column and mix them up. Say each word once and ask them to write it down.

3 Ask the class to work in pairs, telling each other what they think about each item of food or drink in 1–7, using the phrases in the *Key speaking* box.

Listening

4 **1 10** Ask students to look at the photo and the exercise. They are going to hear a boy called Jack and a girl called Katie talking about food and drink. The class should read through the questions. Check that they understand the vocabulary. Explain that you will play the recording twice. The first time they should just listen and the second time they should write down J for Jack or K for Katie next to each question. There is one question where both J and K are needed.

Recording script
Katie: Hi, Jack! It's twelve thirty. Come and have lunch with me! I'm really hungry today.
Jack: Hi, Katie! So am I. I eat lots for breakfast every morning but I still eat a lot for lunch too. What about you, what do you usually have for breakfast?
Katie: Nothing much. My mum makes breakfast at seven o'clock and that's too early for me! I always get a cake or something on my way to school so I don't feel hungry during lessons.
Jack: And then you have chips or pizza for lunch?
Katie: Yes, nearly every day. I love them!
Jack: They're not very good for you, are they? I try to eat a lot of salad. It's healthy. And I drink lots of water. It's better for you than juice.
Katie: I don't like salad very much, and I don't like water. And I think tea and coffee taste horrible. I prefer cola or lemonade.
Jack: I guess you like chocolate as well, don't you? I love chocolate.
Katie: Mmm, I love it too, and sweets and biscuits. But I don't like ice cream very much. It makes my teeth too cold!

5 Students should take a piece of paper and walk around the class to find out what four people like or don't like. Alternatively the class can do this in groups of four, with one person from each group reporting to the class the group's likes and dislikes.

Grammar

6 Students should complete the table with the correct forms of the present simple. Refer students to the section in the Grammar folder on page 137 if they need extra help. The exercise in the Grammar folder can be done in class or for homework.

Answers	
affirmative	I/You/We/They like
	He/She/It likes
negative	I/You/We/They don't like
	He/She/It doesn't like
question	Do I/you/we/they like
	Does he/she/it like

7

Answers
don't   hasn't   haven't   isn't   aren't

8   Ask the class to match the times with the clocks.

Answers
1 c   2 f   3 a   4 d   5 e   6 b

9   *Key* Listening Part 5

1 🔢 Listening Part 5 tests the ability to listen to a monologue containing information – spelling of names, places, times, etc. – and write down the missing information.

Elicit from the class the times when they normally eat their main meals.

Background information

People in Britain usually have breakfast between 7 and 8 o'clock. Breakfast in Britain is usually toast or cereal. British people rarely eat a full cooked breakfast of sausage, bacon, tomatoes, mushrooms and eggs nowadays, except perhaps at weekends.
Lunch is between 12.30 and 1.30. It is often a sandwich or salad, but may be something cooked.
Dinner is from 6.30 to 8.00. It is often meat or fish with potatoes and other vegetables.

Ask students to read through the table. Check they understand the vocabulary. Tell them they will hear a man talking about his day and they should fill the spaces with the missing word or words. Play the recording once to get a general understanding and then again so students can write/check their answers.

Answers
1   orange juice
2   1.15 / one fifteen / a quarter past one
3   water
4   6.30 / six thirty / half past six
5   fish
6   (a cup of) coffee

Recording script
Harry: What do I usually eat and drink? Well, I get up about seven thirty, have a shower and then have breakfast about eight o'clock. I make a cup of tea, and then I have toast and <u>orange juice</u>. Then, I go to my office – I work in advertising. I don't eat snacks, so I'm quite hungry by lunchtime. I have lunch at <u>one fifteen</u>. I have about an hour for lunch, and I often go to a café near my office. I have salad and I sometimes have a cake – the café does fantastic chocolate cakes. And to drink? Well, <u>water</u>. I don't like to have too much tea or coffee in the day. I get home from work about five thirty. I have my evening meal at about <u>six thirty</u> and I like cooking, so I try to make something healthy and interesting – usually chicken or <u>fish</u> with rice or pasta. I never have a dessert, but I do have <u>a cup of coffee</u> then. Then I often go out – maybe to the cinema or with friends. I'm usually in bed by ten thirty during the week.

Activity

Ask the students to look at the questionnaire on page 130. They should walk around the class and ask three students the questions. This will practise the 'I'and 'you' forms of the present tense. They should write down the students' names and their answers.
The students should now have a completed questionnaire. They must ask different students about one of the people they have talked to. So, if a student has talked to, say, Paolo, then another student should ask them about Paolo's routine in order to elicit the 'he/she' forms of the present tense.

3.2 Food at festivals
SB pages 22–23

Background information

Buñol is a town near Valencia in Spain. Every year, on the last Wednesday in August, there is a festival, when people come to throw tomatoes at each other. The festival began in 1945, probably as a joke. The festival has continued off and on until the present day. Some years it was banned by the town council as it became more of a riot than a festival, but it has become so popular that now it happens every year. The festival is highly organised and regulated.

1   Invite students to look at, and comment on, the photograph of the Tomato Festival in Buñol. Possible questions:
What are the people doing?
Why are they doing it?
Would you like to be there? Why? / Why not?
Do you know of other festivals like this one?

Reading

2 **Key Reading Part 4**

This exercise is preparation for Reading Part 4, but here students are only asked to choose between 'Right' and 'Wrong'. Ask students to read the text and try to answer the questions. Tell them not to worry about words they don't know at this stage. They should underline in pencil the word or phrase which they think gives the answer.

Students should then discuss their answers to the questions in pairs. Check to make sure they understand the vocabulary.

Answers
1 Wrong 2 Wrong 3 Right 4 Wrong 5 Wrong
6 Wrong 7 Wrong 8 Right

Grammar extra

3 Students should read through the explanation and do the exercise.

Answers
2 My mother *usually* makes cakes on Tuesdays.
3 I am *always* hungry at lunchtime.
4 I am *often* late for dinner.
5 Pete *always* has a party on his birthday.
6 We *sometimes* have fireworks on New Year's Eve.
7 Sam *usually* meets his friends on New Year's Eve.
8 You *never* eat spaghetti with a knife.

Grammar

4 Klara is a girl from Sweden. She is talking about an important festival in Sweden called Santa Lucia Day. Ask the students to read through the text. Make sure they understand all the vocabulary – words such as 'candle' and 'crown' might be new to them. Then the students should decide on the correct forms of the verbs in brackets.

Answers
1 have 2 wear 3 carry 4 wears 5 wakes
6 help 7 often ask 8 aren't 9 don't wear
10 choose 11 sing 12 like 13 always closes

5 Ask students to work in pairs or groups to discuss what they do on their special days. Put new vocabulary on the board. Check that they are using adverbs of frequency correctly and that they remember to put an -s/-es on the end of third person singular verbs in the present simple.

Extension activity

Explain that students are going to talk about differences between the UK and their own country. Give each student a copy of the fact sheet about the UK from the Teacher's Audio CD/CD-ROM. They then have to discuss what differences there are between their country and the UK. One person in each group writes down the differences. At the end, each group feeds back to the rest of the class.

6 **Key Writing Part 9**

There are five marks for Writing Part 9 in the exam. Candidates are not expected to write perfect English. However, they must communicate all three parts of the message. Do not treat this as an exam task, but encourage students to mention all three points in their answer.

Sample answer
Dear Maria,
We have a special festival in our town on 14th July for Independence Day. We have fireworks in the evening and we have wonderful cakes and sweet biscuits.
Love,
Paula

Activity

Encourage students to use the following language:
* *When were you born?*
* *What's/When's your birthday?*
* *Were you born in November? What date?*
* *My birthday is the 12th of December.*

Writing folder 1

SB pages 24–25

Writing Part 6 Spelling words

Ask students to read the information about this part of the Reading and Writing paper. It is important to give them plenty of practice in spelling to prepare them for this part of the exam. There are Part 6 practice tasks for every unit on pages 154–158 of the Student's Book.

Extension activity

Play a game to help students with their spelling. One person thinks of a word and puts dashes for each letter on the board. The class have to guess the missing letters. If they guess wrong, then a line is drawn to form a cat: (1st wrong letter – draw the head, 2nd – an ear, 3rd – another ear, 4th – the body, 5th – a paw, 6th – another paw, 7th – the tail, and finally six whiskers (one wrong letter each).
The winner is the first person to guess the word. If nobody guesses the word before the cat is complete, the person who thought of the word is the winner.

1 When the students have finished this matching task, you could ask them to write a similar list of beginnings and endings of words for their partner to do.

Answers
2 butter 3 waitress 4 dish 5 juice 6 market
7 pasta 8 tomato 9 carrot 10 apple

2 Ask the students to work through the exercise in pairs and decide which word is spelled wrongly. They may use an English–English dictionary to help them.

Answers
2 pilot
3 yellow
4 mirror
5 uncle
6 beautiful
7 telephone
8 sunny
9 which
10 interesting
11 believe
12 apartment
13 motorbike
14 because
15 address
16 bicycle

3 This exercise practises definitions.

Possible answers
2 This food is very popular in Italy.
3 I will bring you your food in a restaurant.
4 This is where you can go to eat lunch.
5 This is the first meal of the day.
6 This is something small you can eat between meals.
7 This is where you cook food.
8 This keeps food cold.
9 An apple is an example of this.
10 This is good to eat on a hot day.

4 The students should spend some time either in class or for homework writing their own definitions for their partner to guess.

Students should read through the Exam advice carefully. Check they understand each point. Care needs to be taken as some answers could be plural. Get students into the habit of checking to see whether the answer will be plural before they do the exercise.

Next to the Exam advice there is an example of an answer sheet. Make sure the students know how to fill it in. Marks are often lost because the answer sheet is wrongly completed.

Part 6

Answers
1 lemonade
2 tomatoes
3 orange
4 sugar
5 sandwiches

4 The past

Preparation

Make one copy of the recording script on the Teacher's Audio CD/CD–ROM (Photocopiable activities, page 5) for each student. This will be used in 4.2.

4.1 A real adventure
SB pages 26–27

1 Ask the students to work in pairs or groups to talk about the statements 1–5. They should try to guess the answers if they aren't sure.

Answers
1 Right – it is often used to decorate cakes.
2 Wrong – they are mainly made from silver and covered with gold.
3 Wrong – most gold comes from China today.
4 Right – in the engines
5 Right – the photo shows a wedding dress made from gold thread designed by Yumi Katsura.

Reading

2 **Key** Reading Part 4

Reading Part 4 can be either a Right, Wrong, Doesn't say or a multiple-choice task. The questions are always given in the same order as the information occurs in the text. The best way for students to tackle a Right, Wrong, Doesn't say task is to go through the questions, answering 'Right' or 'Wrong' where they can, and underlining the part of the text that tells them the answer. They should then go back through the remaining questions and check that there is no

information in the text to answer them, in which case they answer 'Doesn't say'. Stress to students that they should not use their own knowledge to answer the questions. For 'Right' and 'Wrong' answers the information must be found in the text, and if not, the answer has to be 'Doesn't say'.

Answers
1 Wrong
2 Right
3 Wrong
4 Doesn't say
5 Wrong
6 Doesn't say
7 Right

Grammar

3 This should be revision of the past simple tense. If students require more practice, they should look in the Grammar folder. There is an additional exercise on that page that they can do in class or for homework.

Answers
1 wanted
2 worked
3 found
4 became
5 was; were

Where **did** the Canadian Skookum Jim **find** gold?

But some people **didn't** (did not) **go** only for the gold, they went for the adventure too.

Spelling spot

4 First, go through the explanation with students and check they understand the rules.

Answers
1 arrived
2 stopped
3 helped
4 looked
5 used
6 returned
7 liked
8 played
9 studied
10 chatted

Pronunciation

5 **1 12** The focus is on the sounds /t/ as in *tent* and /d/ as in *duck*. Draw students' attention to the pictures. These are the sounds that are made in the regular past simple verb endings.

Students should underline the regular verbs in the past simple. They should then work in pairs and decide how the ending of each verb is pronounced. It might be a good idea to do a few for practice first. For example:

/t/ *talked*
/d/ *lived*
/ɪd/ *decided*

When students have completed the exercise, they should listen to the recording to check their answers.

Recording script and answers

/t/	/d/	/ɪd/
worked	carried	wanted
picked	showed	decided
	travelled	needed
	stayed	

6 Explain that not all verbs are regular. For a list of irregular verbs, see page 159 of the Student's Book.

Answers
1 found 2 saw 3 knew 4 sold 5 left 6 built
7 went 8 became 9 spent

Activity

1 13 The class should listen to the recording and then try to guess who the person is. They should then play the game themselves, possibly first as a class and then in small groups. They should ask a maximum of 12 to 15 questions.

Recording script
Boy: Are you ready to play?
Girl: Yes, I'm ready.
Boy: Were you a man?
Girl: Yes, I was.
Boy: Were you American?
Girl: No, I wasn't.
Boy: Were you European?
Girl: Yes, I was.
Boy: So, dead, man and European. Did you live more than a hundred years ago?
Girl: Yes, I did.
Boy: Were you Italian?
Girl: Yes, I was.
Boy: Did you play music?
Girl: No, I didn't.

Boy: Were you a writer?
Girl: No, I wasn't.
Boy: Did you paint pictures?
Girl: Yes, I did.
Boy: Were you …?

Answers
The famous person is Leonardo da Vinci.

4.2 A mini-adventure
SB pages 28–29

1 Tell students about an interesting place you went to last year – or make one up! Students should work in pairs and ask and answer the questions in the exercise. Tell them they can make up the answers if they want to.

Check that students are forming the questions correctly, i.e.
Where did you go / stay?
When did you go / come home?
How much did it cost?
How did you travel / feel?
What did you do / see / buy?
What did you see?
Who did you go with?
How long did you stay?

Listening

2 Key Listening Part 5

1 14 In Part 5 of the Listening paper, students will hear a monologue and they will need to write down information such as numbers, places, names, etc. It is a good idea to practise spelling out words aloud for this part of the test.

Ask students to look at the photos and talk about them.

The second photo was taken in the Louvre museum in Paris and the bottom photo is of a bateau mouche (a special sightseeing boat which cruises along the River Seine in Paris) with Notre Dame cathedral in the background. Then play the recording and ask students to circle the correct answer.

Answers

1 5
2 5.30
3 £340
4 BERRI
5 boat trip

Recording script

Melanie: About two years ago I went with my class on our first school trip – <u>five days</u> in Paris! There were about thirty of us and four teachers. We all went in one big coach from our school in London. The teachers told us to be at school at four thirty in the morning. Everyone was there on time, but the coach didn't arrive until five o'clock and <u>we didn't leave until five thirty</u>! We were very cold and tired.

Anyway, the coach was very comfortable and we watched a DVD and listened to some music on the journey. We had some sandwiches and drinks with us, so we went straight to Paris without stopping. The trip was quite expensive. <u>It cost £340</u> and we wanted to save money, so we didn't stop at motorway cafés. It only took us eight hours to reach Paris.

The name of the hotel in Paris was <u>the Hotel Berri – that's B-E-double R-I</u>. It was very old, but our room was nice and the bed was great – really soft! I shared the room with three other girls.

When we went shopping I tried to practise my French a few times but sometimes I didn't know the right words and spoke in English instead! The shops were great – I bought lots of presents, even a T-shirt for my little sister!

I think <u>what I enjoyed most was the boat trip</u>. I took lots of photos of my friends and also of Notre Dame cathedral, and the wonderful art galleries.

I was sad to leave Paris. I had a lovely time there. We came home by coach and this time the journey was much shorter – we even arrived back half an hour early!

3 Ask students to read through the questions. Play the recording again, and ask the class to write down the answers. They may need to hear the recording once more. They should check their answers in pairs.

Answers

2 Yes, she did.
3 Yes, it did.
4 No, they didn't.
5 No, she didn't.
6 Yes, she did.
7 No, they didn't.

P hotocopiable recording script activity ◎

Hand out copies of the recording script from the Teacher's Audio CD/CD-ROM (Photocopiable activities page 5). Ask students to work in pairs. They should underline the answers for exercise 3.
Now ask the class to underline all the descriptive adjectives in the recording script. They should then use a dictionary to find the opposite of each adjective.

Answers

first – last	great – awful
big – small/little	soft – hard
cold – hot	right – wrong
tired – energetic	little – big
comfortable – uncomfortable	wonderful – terrible
expensive – cheap	sad – happy
old – new	lovely – horrible
nice – horrible	shorter – longer

Grammar extra

4 Go through the examples of the use of *ago* in the box. Explain that we use *ago* to talk about a certain time period in the past. Explain that the other expressions in the box below – *yesterday, at breakfast,* etc. – are more precise times.

Go round the class asking questions so that they understand the difference between a period of time and an exact time. Flashcards would be useful for this: one with *ago*, one with *at the weekend*, etc., so it could be held up and the student has to answer with that time expression.

Ask students to do the exercise in pairs.

Possible questions and answers

1 When did you last eat some chocolate?
   I ate some chocolate three hours ago.
2 When did you last email a friend?
   I emailed a friend two days ago.
3 When did you last read a magazine?
   I read a magazine last night.
4 When did you last listen to music?
   I listened to music twelve hours ago.
5 When did you last go to the cinema?
   I went to the cinema two weeks ago.
6 When did you last play football?
   I played football yesterday. / I don't play football.
7 When did you last do some homework?
   I did some homework at breakfast time.
8 When did you last go to an art gallery?
   I went to an art gallery last weekend.
9 When did you last buy some clothes?
   I bought some clothes on Saturday.
10 When did you last eat pizza?
   I ate pizza at lunchtime.

5

Answers
1 You didn't *come* home at six o'clock.
2 Who *did you go* to London with?
3 I *laughed* a lot during the game.
4 I *danced* with Louise last night.
5 I *played* football with my brother on Saturday.
6 I *stayed* with my friend yesterday.
7 I *bought* it because I love green.
8 (correct)
9 How much *did the trip cost*?
10 Last Monday, the school *told* us about the new holiday.

Activity

Answers
Across
went   ate   began   travelled
Down
liked   had   took   arrived   saw   stayed

w	e	n	t	b	s	d	e	t	s
l	d	w	t	a	t	a	t	e	t
i	d	d	a	t	k	r	y	u	a
k	s	u	r	o	j	r	j	k	y
e	a	n	g	o	k	i	s	w	e
d	b	t	f	k	t	v	a	d	d
p	u	i	h	f	c	e	w	i	c
b	e	g	a	n	s	d	r	v	x
o	z	a	d	p	d	a	t	u	i
l	t	r	a	v	e	l	l	e	d

Units 1–4 Revision

SB pages 30–31

Speaking

1 Discuss the first sentence and the example answer with the whole class, then let them work through the others in pairs. If appropriate, have a brief whole-class discussion of some of the other sentences and revise any language problems which have arisen as they talked in pairs.

Exercises 2–8 could be set for homework and discussed afterwards in class.

Vocabulary

2 Other answers may be correct depending on how they are justified.

Suggested answers
1 green – not a feeling
2 small – not a character adjective
3 friend – not an adjective
4 house – you can't buy things there
5 coffee – you drink it, not eat it
6 onion – not a fruit
7 chemist – not a geographical feature
8 clothes – something you wear, not something you use

3

Answers
1 tomato
2 snack
3 meat
4 milk
5 juice
6 grape
7 fish
8 carrot
9 burger
10 chocolate
11 potato
12 chicken

Writing

4 Note that in part 6 of the exam, answers are always just one word. Here students are just revising vocabulary from Units 1–4

Answers
1 market   2 department store   3 chemist
4 supermarket   5 sports shop

Grammar

5

Answers
1 some   2 much   3 is   4 any   5 Does   6 Sometimes
7 doesn't   8 go   9 Did   10 return

6

Answers
1 starts   2 a   3 make   4 their   5 eat   6 some
7 at   8 Many   9 wear   10 is

7

Answers
1 knew
2 came
3 found
4 sold
5 took
6 told
7 became
8 left
9 went
10 built

8

Answers
2 am/'m
3 telephoned
4 were
5 needed
6 went
7 Did you get
8 do you think
9 'm/am not
10 like
11 Are
12 are / 're
13 looked
14 took
15 saw
16 were
17 Were
18 look
19 got
20 were

5 Animals

Preparation

Make copies of the *Collocation Snap* cards on the Teacher's Audio CD/CD-ROM (Photocopiable activities, page 6) and cut them up so that each student has ten cards.

5.1 Going to the zoo
SB pages 32–33

Vocabulary

1   *Key* Writing Part 6

Ask the class to look at the pictures of animals and then do the exercise. The photos show:

1 a horse	**5** a bear
2 a fish	**6** an elephant
3 a cat	**7** a dog
4 a lion	**8** a monkey

Answers
1 bear   2 cat   3 dog   4 elephant   5 horse
6 fish   7 monkey   8 lion

2   This exercise can be done either in groups or as a class discussion.

Listening

3   **1 15** The task here is designed to ease the students gently into a listening comprehension. Ask the class to look at the list of words. Play the recording and ask them to tick the words as they hear them. All the words are mentioned. They are in italics in the recording script below.

Recording script

Mark: Natalie, what about going to the *zoo* at the weekend?

Natalie: Oh, sorry, Mark, but I'm going shopping on Saturday and I'm going to see my grandparents on *Sunday*, but I'm free in the week.

Mark: OK, then let's say Thursday.

Natalie: Fine. It's cheaper then too. At the weekend it's £18.50 for adults and £17.50 for *students*! But in the week student tickets are £3 cheaper.

Mark: Mm, £14.50 – not bad! At the zoo, I've got to take some photographs of the animals for *homework*. My art teacher asked me and a friend to take as many as possible. It's lucky my mum bought me a *camera* for my birthday!

Natalie: Well, there are lots of different animals. My favourites are the lions, bears and monkeys. The monkeys always make me *laugh*.

Mark: Let's visit them first, then. I need some photos of them.

Natalie: OK, so how are we going to get there, Mark? Can your mum *drive* us there?

Mark: She'll be at work then. I think the bus is best, as the *train*'s too expensive. I don't want to spend too much money.

Natalie: Fine, but I need to be home by six thirty.

Mark: Well, that's no problem because it shuts at five thirty. We'll be tired anyway, so why don't we leave at half past *four*?

Natalie: That's *great*! See you soon, then.

Mark: Bye!

4   *Key* Listening Part 3

1 16 In Part 3 of the Listening paper candidates are given five multiple-choice questions on a dialogue that they hear. There is also an example.

Let students read through the example question and possible answers carefully. Play the recording of the example. Point out that although all three days are mentioned on the recording, 'Thursday' is the correct answer to the question.

5   **1 17** Play the next track, which is the rest of Mark and Natalie's conversation, and let students answer the questions. The answers are underlined in the recording script above.

Answers
1 A 2 C 3 B 4 A 5 B

6 Ask the students to work in pairs and ask and answer the questions.

Grammar extra

7 Refer students to the explanation in the Student's Book. Ask them to do the error correction exercise.

Possible questions and answers
1 I saw a nice, colourful parrot at the zoo.
2 Yesterday we went to the zoo and the museum.
3 Susanna went out yesterday and took her dog for a walk.
4 There are many cats, dogs and horses at the farm.
5 Some sheep and cows were at the farm.

Vocabulary

8 Explain that some words in English go together. We call these collocations. Refer to the example, which is taken from the recording.

Ask the class to work through the exercise in pairs. One noun can be used more than once.

Answers
do – homework, the shopping, nothing, the cooking
make – a phone call, an appointment, a cake
take – the dog for a walk, an exam
spend – time, nothing
Make time and *take a phone call* are also possible collocations, but students at this level would not be expected to know them.

9 This exercise can be done in class or for homework.

Answers
1 spent 2 did 3 did 4 make 5 took

Extension activity ◉

Collocation Snap
Copy and cut up the *Collocation Snap* cards on the Teacher's Audio CD/CD-ROM (Photocopiable activities, page 6) and give each student ten cards.

The cards are a mixture of verbs and nouns. The verbs are *do, take, make, spend* and *have*. The nouns are *homework, photographs, a cake, some money, a shower, a party, a cold, breakfast, a drink, a picture, a phone call, nothing, an appointment* and *time*.

Students play in pairs. They put their cards in a pile, face down. They take it in turns to turn over their top card. If it collocates with the card their partner has just turned over, they get a point if they can say a sentence using the collocation.

10 Students form pairs and discuss the questions using the collocations they have learnt.

5.2 An amazing animal
SB pages 34–35

1 Tell students to cover the text on polar bears at the bottom of the page and work through the quiz in pairs, discussing whether the answers are a) or b).

Reading

2 Check for understanding and any unknown vocabulary.

Answers to the quiz in exercise 1
1 a 2 b 3 a 4 a 5 a 6 b 7 b 8 b 9 a

Grammar

3 Refer students to the underlined examples in the text. There is an additional exercise in the Grammar folder on page 140 of the Student's Book that they can do for homework or in class.

Answers
We use *because, and, but* and *or* to make one long sentence.
1 because
2 or
3 and
4 but

4 **Key Reading Part 5**

In Reading Part 5, students read through a text and identify the appropriate structural word (auxiliary, modal, determiner, pronoun, preposition, conjunction, etc.) that is gapped. There are eight three-option multiple-choice questions plus an integrated example.

Answers
1 B because 2 A and 3 A or 4 B because
5 A or 6 C but 7 A because

5 Students decide which conjunction to use to join each sentence together: *and, or, but* or *because*. In some of these examples a case can be made for one or more of the alternatives.

Answers
1 and/but 2 because 3 but 4 or/and/but
5 because

Extension activity

Ask the class to work in groups. Each group chooses an animal. They must write down sentences about their animal. For example:

I huve u dog. I take her for walks because she needs exercise. I feed her meat and give her water to drink. She also likes chocolate chips or biscuits to eat. She likes playing with me, but not with my cat.

When students have finished, they should read out their sentences to the class. They get a point for each correct sentence.

Spelling spot

6   These words are often confused by students at this level. Go through the examples and ask the class to do the exercise.

Answers
1 They're   2 there   3 their   4 Their   5 They're
6 there

7

Sample answer
Dear Lucia,
I went to a great zoo in London last weekend with my friend Caroline and her family. We saw lots of animals but I liked the lions best. We had ice cream and juice and took lots of photographs.
Love from
Sandro

Pronunciation

8   **1 18** Play the recording of the examples in the Student's Book. Emphasise the falling intonation on the last word of a list.

Let students practise in pairs, checking each other's intonation.

Activity

This exercise recycles vocabulary and intonation. Remind students to use the listing intonation they have just practised in the Pronunciation exercise. Start off the game by saying: *I went to the zoo and I saw a lion.*

Zoo animals that the students could use are the following:
bear, elephant, lion, monkey, snake, horse, insect.
Words they may know but which are B1 are:
butterfly, camel, dolphin, donkey, giraffe, goat, kangaroo, parrot, penguin, spider, tiger.

Exam folder 3

SB pages 36–37

Reading Part 2 Multiple choice

1   Ask the students to read the information about this
    part of the Reading and Writing paper. They should
    then decide which of the words in each category is
    wrong. For example, *horse* is a noun, not a verb.

> **Answers**
> verbs – *go, made, carry, <u>horse</u>*
> nouns – *<u>left</u>, house, dog, teacher*
> adjectives – *happy, <u>sun</u>, nice, friendly*
> adverbs – *hard, slowly, <u>want</u>, carefully*
> words which go together – *have breakfast, <u>make</u> your
> homework, take a trip*

Give students time to read through the Exam advice and
check for understanding. Draw their attention to the
sample answer sheet and make sure they know how to fill
it in correctly.

Ask students to do the Part 2 task. Explain that there is
only one correct answer. Use the example question (o) to
show why **B** is the answer. This is because the verb *enjoy* is
followed by an *-ing* form, but *want* and *agree* are not:
Rebecca and Tom <u>want to visit</u> their uncle's farm.
Rebecca and Tom <u>agree to visit</u> their uncle's farm.

> **Answers**
> **6** A   **7** B   **8** C   **9** B   **10** A

Ask the students to write sentences showing how the
other words are used.

Reading Part 5 Multiple-choice cloze

For this part of the exam, students read a text with eight
three-option multiple-choice questions. There is also an
example.

2   Ask the students to look at the types of word which
    are tested. They should match parts of speech 1–7 with
    examples a–g.

> **Answers**
> **1** c   **2** d   **3** e   **4** f   **5** g   **6** a   **7** b

Ask the students to do the Part 5 task. When they have
finished they should compare answers with a partner and
justify their decisions. Again, students might find it useful
to write a sentence showing how the wrong options are
used.

> **Answers**
> **28** C   **29** A   **30** B   **31** A   **32** B   **33** A   **34** C   **35** A

6 Leisure and hobbies

6.1 Theme park fun

SB pages 38–39

Speaking

1   Invite the class to look at the photos of the rides at different theme parks. Ask them to discuss, in pairs, which one they prefer and then go on to talk about theme parks in general.

2   Ask students to consider all the information in the leaflets and discuss in pairs which park they would like to go to. Open this up to a class discussion – this activity should only take 5–10 minutes at most.

3   **Key Speaking Part 2**

The usual format for the Speaking test is two candidates and two examiners. One examiner, the interlocutor, will ask the questions and the other examiner, the assessor, will write down the marks. Part 2 lasts about 3–4 minutes and during that time the candidates will talk to each other. They will be given cards with prompt material containing factual information of a non-personal kind.

This exercise is initial practice for Part 2 of the Speaking test. In the test itself, the candidates cannot see each other's cards.

Ask students to form pairs and decide who is Student A and who is Student B.
Student A should ask Student B questions about Magic Land.
Student B should ask Student A questions about Space Adventure.
They should answer using the information in the leaflets.

4   Students should work through this exercise, which is the introduction to comparative adjectives.

Possible questions
1   How many rides does Magic Land / Space Adventure have?
2   Which dates is Magic Land / Space Adventure open on?
3   What are the opening hours of Magic Land / Space Adventure?
4   How many visitors does Magic Land / Space Adventure have a year?
5   How many hotel rooms does Magic Land / Space Adventure have?
6   How much does Magic Land / Space Adventure cost?

Grammar

Answers
1 newer   2 shorter   3 smaller   4 more
5 more   6 better   7 less

5   Students should find examples in exercise 4 to fill in the gaps in this exercise. This will provide them with the basic rules of how to form a comparative adjective.

Answers
1/2 older, newer, longer, shorter, bigger, smaller
3   more/less expensive
4   better
5   worse
6   than
7   more
8   fewer

Reading

6   Ask students if they know which theme parks are the biggest and best in the world. They should then read the text to see if their park is mentioned.

Grammar

7 The words underlined in the text in exercise 6 are superlative adjectives. Ask students to use the information in the reading text to complete exercise 7 with superlative adjectives. Refer them to the Grammar folder on page 140 of the Student's Book for an additional exercise. This can be done in class or for homework.

Answers
1 the oldest amusement park
2 the tallest rollercoaster
3 the fastest rollercoaster

Extension activity

Ask students to make as many words in English as they can out of the letters in the word 'rollercoaster'. They can use an English–English dictionary to help them. The student with the most words, and who can explain what they all mean, wins.

Spelling spot

8 Check students understand the rules and ask them to complete the chart.

Answers

comparative	superlative
more modern	the most modern
more comfortable	the most comfortable
fitter	the fittest
more horrible	the most horrible
angrier	the angriest
more attractive	the most attractive
brighter	the brightest
tidier	the tidiest

Extension activity

Ask the class to form groups of four to six.
Everyone in the group has to form a line according to the instructions they are given. For example: *Form a line according to how long your hair is. The person with the shortest hair goes at the front.*
The winners are the team who form a line correctly in the shortest time. Each person in the team must be able to say a correct sentence in English using a comparative or superlative adjective, e.g. *My hair is longer than Sarah's. Jean's got the shortest hair*, etc. If they can't do this, their team is disqualified.
Students can do this activity to talk about:
– size of feet
– size of pet / number of pets
– number of brothers and sisters in family
– height

6.2 Free time
SB pages 40–41

Speaking

1 Students should work in pairs to discuss the questions. Then they should look at the pictures and ask and answer questions about other things they do in their free time.

Listening

2 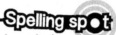 *Key* Listening Part 4

1 **19** Listening Part 4 is similar to Part 5, in that both are gap-fill exercises. However, Part 4 is a conversation whereas Part 5 is a monologue.

Ask students to predict the sorts of words the answers will be in this exercise. For example: Is the answer to 1 a number or a word? Is it a price or a time? What do you think the missing word is in 4? What do cafés sell?

This may seem very easy to do, but it is worth pointing out to students that it would be very helpful for them to do this in the exam, as it will give them some idea of what they are listening for.

Answers
1 10 (p.m.)   2 (£)55   3 Glendennan   4 ice cream
5 books

Recording script
Man: Hello, Aqua Park. Can I help you?
Girl: Yes, please. I'd like some information. Are you open on Saturdays?
Man: We're open every day. From nine in the morning until six, but on Saturdays we close much later, at ten.
Girl: OK. And how much does it cost?
Man: Adults are £20 and children £15, but families can get in more cheaply with a family ticket – only £55.
Girl: And do you have a large car park? I'm coming from London.
Man: We have four car parks. From London it's much easier for you to park in the one in Glendennan Road.
Girl: I'll write that down. Can you spell the name of the road for me?
Man: It's G-L-E-N-D-E-double N-A-N.
Girl: And is there anywhere to get food and drink?
Man: Yes, there's a restaurant for hot food. There's also a café for ice cream and drinks.
Girl: Is there anything else I need to know? Do you have a shop?
Man: Yes. It sells sweets, newspapers, and you can get books there, too.
Girl: That's great. Thank you.

Extension activity

Students need lots of practice at listening to words being spelt out. The letters G/J, B/V/P, N/M, A/E/I, W/U/Y are particularly hard to hear. They also need to practise numbers, especially 14/40, 15/50, etc.

Ask students to choose a place that they go to in their free time – a swimming pool, shop, cinema, etc. They should write down as much information about the place as they can, e.g. opening times, address, what type of place it is. Students can change the information slightly if the places are too well known.

Now ask them to write down a list of questions they might want to ask, e.g.
* *Where is it?*
* *What does it sell?*
* *When does it open/close?*

Students then form pairs and ask and answer questions about their place. If Student A doesn't know the answer to a question, he or she can say 'I don't know'. Student B is allowed to ask Student A to repeat the answer or to spell the word aloud.

Grammar extra

If students aren't sure what the difference is between an adjective and an adverb, remind them that adjectives give extra information about nouns, whereas adverbs give extra information about verbs. For example:

The car goes *fast* (adverb). It's a *fast* (adjective) car. It goes *faster* (comparative adverb) than yours. It's a *faster* (comparative adjective) car than yours.

I worked *hard* (adverb) today. I'm a *hard* (adjective) worker. I worked *harder* (comparative adverb) than you did. I'm the *hardest* (superlative adjective) worker in the class.

3   Students should complete the exercise either in class or at home.

Answers
1 sooner   2 harder   3 more quietly   4 earlier
5 longer   6 better   7 more carefully

4   *Key* Writing Part 9

These mistakes are taken from *Key* exam scripts and are the most common ones that are made at this level. Although a few spelling errors are acceptable in the exam, it is better to keep these to a minimum. It may be a good idea to make a poster and put up words which the class has trouble spelling, so that they are there as a constant reminder.

Answers
friend   beautiful   because   interesting   there   which

Reading

5   *Key* Reading Part 2

Ask the students to read through each sentence to get an idea of what the story is about. They should then either work alone or in pairs to decide on the right answer. After checking the answers with the students, go through the other options and talk about why they are wrong.

Answers
1 C   2 B   3 C   4 B   5 A

Pronunciation

6   **1 20** The focus is on the unstressed vowel sound /ə/, as at the end of *camera*. Draw students' attention to the picture. Then ask them to listen and repeat.

7   Check that students understand how a crossword puzzle works and that *Across* and *Down* are clear instructions. This could be done at home or in class. Check that students pronounce the answers clearly.

Answers

Across	Down
1 alone	2 listen
6 computer	3 camera
9 interesting	4 longer
10 America	5 father
	7 cinema
	8 letter

Activity

Divide the class into two groups, A and B. Group A is going to ask questions about free-time activities at home. Group B is going to ask questions about free-time physical activities. Students should use the questionnaires on page 131 of their Student's Books.

Give students some time to read their questionnaire and write a few more questions. Students should then go round the class asking the questions to students from the other group. In order to find out how many people do the activity, they will need to put a tick next to the question to represent each person.

When they have completed their questionnaires, ask them to report back to the class, using comparatives and superlatives where possible. For example:
Most people watch TV every night.
The largest number of people go swimming.
People think chess is the least interesting game.
More people like playing computer games than watching TV.

Exam folder 4

SB pages 42–43

Listening Parts 4 and 5
Gap-fill

Ask students to read the information about Parts 4 and 5 of the Listening paper.

Ask the students to work in pairs to do the introductory exercise. Student A should give Student B the information and spell out any words that are necessary. Student B should write the information down.

Remind students that when saying telephone numbers, o is pronounced *oh* and 33 is pronounced *double three*. With dates we write *1st August* and we say *the first of August*.

Refer the class to the Exam advice box and check they understand the information.

Part 4

1 21 Students should have a quick look through the questions to get an idea of what they are listening for. There is no extra time given for this in the exam. Part 4 is a conversation between two people.

> **Answers**
> **16** eleven/11
> **17** £300
> **18** Kensal – this must be spelled correctly
> **19** eighteen/18
> **20** nine thirty / 9.30 / half past nine

Recording script

Questions 16 to 20. You will hear a woman asking about a guitar for sale. Listen and complete questions 16 to 20. You will hear the conversation twice.

Man: 669872.

Woman: Oh, hello. I'm ringing about the guitar you have for sale. Can you tell me what make it is?

Man: It's a <u>Fender</u>.

Woman: And how old is it?

Man: Well, I bought it from a friend about six months ago, and he was given it for his birthday, so it's about <u>eleven</u> months old now.

Woman: How much are you selling it for?

Man: Umm, I think I'd like <u>three hundred</u> pounds for it. I bought it for six hundred.

Woman: Sounds good. Can I come and see it?

Man: Sure. I live at 60, Kensal Road. That's <u>K-E-N-S-A-L</u> Road.

Woman: Can I walk there from the High Street?

Man: It's probably best if you get a bus. The number <u>eighteen</u> bus stops in my road outside number seventy.

Woman: I'm free tonight. Would about eight o'clock be OK?

Man: A bit later? After <u>nine thirty</u> is better for me as I don't get back from work until eight.

Woman: My name is Jenny Levine and you are …?

Man: Josh Bentley.

Woman: See you tonight, then.

Now listen again.

(The recording is repeated.)

Part 5

1 22 Ask students to look at Part 5. They should try to predict the answers. Part 5 is a monologue.

> **Answers**
> **21** tennis
> **22** £425
> **23** 18
> **24** Wright – this must be spelled correctly
> **25** 8775980

Recording script

Questions 21 to 25. You will hear some information about an activity centre. Listen and complete questions 21 to 25. You will hear the information twice.

Woman: Thank you for calling High Cross Activity Centre. The Centre is open from <u>March to October</u> and we have things to do for all ages. At High Cross you can play football or try our new climbing wall, and you can also learn to play <u>tennis</u>. It costs £35 to come for a day and for this you get your classes and lunch in our restaurant. One week's stay is <u>£425</u> for a room and all meals. It is cheaper if you come here as part of a group. We are happy to accept group bookings, especially from companies and schools. Group sizes can be from five to <u>eighteen</u> people. If you would like to talk about what we do here, then ring our manager, Pete Wright, that's <u>W-R-I-G-H-T</u>. Office hours are nine o'clock until five thirty and the number to ring is <u>8775980</u>. After five thirty you can ring Pete's mobile on 0770 5566328.

Now listen again.

(The recording is repeated.)

7 Clothes

7.1 The latest fashion	
Exam skills	Reading Part 4: Multiple choice – three short articles
Grammar	Simple and continuous tenses
Spelling	-ing form
7.2 Your clothes	
Vocabulary	Clothes; adjectives to describe clothes
Listening	Listening for specific information
Pronunciation	The last letters of the alphabet: *w, x, y, z*
Exam skills	Reading Part 3: Short conversations
Preparation	

You will need a hat and dice for each team of six students for the Activity in 7.2.

7.1 The latest fashion
SB pages 44–45

1 Ask students to do this warm-up activity in small groups, encouraging them to use the sentence openers given. Elicit information about their favourite T-shirts, baseball caps, etc.

Reading

2 **Key Reading Part 4**

This gist question encourages students to skim the three short articles for general meaning before looking at the questions.

Answers
Converse boots are the oldest: T-shirts – 1940s
Converse boots – 1917   baseball cap – 1954

3 Explain that in a Reading Part 4 task of this type students need to read the questions carefully and match the content to one of the three articles, choosing A, B or C. Warn students that there will be some 'distraction' for each question in the other articles. Full advice for this part is given in Exam folder 10 on page 116.

Answers
1 A   2 C   3 B   4 C   5 B   6 A   7 B

Grammar

4 Ask students to read the example sentences in the timeline and fill in the missing dates. Note that two different tenses are used in the sentences (the past simple and past continuous) but don't point this out to students until exercise 5.

Answers
1 1954
2 1955
3 1959

5 Ask students to identify the tense of each underlined verb and elicit reasons for why the two different tenses are used in sentence 3. Refer them to the notes in the Grammar folder on page 140 if necessary.

Answers
1 the present continuous (temporary)
2 the present simple (habitual)
3 the past continuous (was wearing = temporary in the past) and past simple (fell = completed action)

6 This exercise focuses on forming the past continuous. Make sure students give you both affirmative and negative sentences.

7 Ask students to fill in the missing verbs in the timeline in pairs and then complete the story.

Answers
Timeline
10.20 – 10.45 was looking at
10.35 saw
10.45 started
10.46 left

Story
2 saw
3 was trying on
4 decided
5 said
6 went
7 found
8 was waiting
9 started
10 left

8 This exercise provides further practice in past tenses. If time is short, the sentences can be set for homework.

Answers
1 were selling
2 bought
3 was watching; rang
4 was wearing; stopped; changed
5 was waiting; drove; gave
6 was living; heard

Spelling spot

Explain that the -ing form of many verbs requires a spelling change. Ask students to look at the examples carefully.

9 Ask students to write the -ing forms on their own. Students can then take turns to write their answers on the board.

Answers

break	breaking
leave	leaving
make	making
throw	throwing
stay	staying
lend	lending
sit	sitting
win	winning

7.2 Your clothes
SB pages 46–47
Vocabulary

1 Elicit answers round the class.

Answers
1 boots
2 hat(s)
3 belt(s)
4 sweater
5 tights
6 suit
7 baseball cap(s)
8 jacket
9 jeans
10 shirt
11 trainers
12 skirt
13 shoes
14 shorts
15 socks
16 trousers
17 ring
18 scarf
19 earrings
20 necklace

2 Elicit answers. These are useful phrases for students to know, as they are very common and can be used in a number of situations.

Answers
A pair of describes things that are used together (e.g. socks, shoes), sometimes referring to plural nouns (e.g. scissors, trousers). *A couple of* means two of something, not necessarily identical things.
Pictures 1, 5, 9, 11, 13, 14, 15, 16 and 20 show pairs of things.

3 Check understanding of the nouns listed, especially *button, material, pocket*. Ask students to use some of the adjectives and nouns in their descriptions.

Extension activity

Suggest students prepare a class exhibition on clothes and fashion, using vocabulary they have learned in this unit. They can bring in photographs from magazines or research internet websites for information. Organise them into groups and suggest different topics they could prepare – for example, the clothes of a famous designer, today's top fashion models, what clothes are made of, the history of shoes. They should write short texts to go with any pictures, for display on the classroom wall.

Listening

4 **1 23** This listening task practises the general skill of listening for specific information. Play the recording twice if necessary. Ask students to put ticks in the table as they listen and then compare answers in pairs.

Answers
Speaker 1, Ben:	shorts and (two) T-shirts
Speaker 2, Louisa:	jacket
Speaker 3, Chris:	trousers and cap

Recording script
Speaker 1 Ben: I work as a waiter on Wednesday evenings and I save most of the money I earn. My dad said I should buy some new trousers for work, but yesterday I saw this pair of yellow cotton shorts, with lots of pockets. They looked wonderful, and I decided to get them for the summer, with a couple of extra T-shirts. Dad still thinks I need some trousers, but my boss doesn't mind what I wear!

Speaker 2 Louisa: There was this beautiful Italian leather jacket in the sale. It was soft black leather, with a pocket on each side. I tried it on over a red shirt I was wearing at the time, and it looked so cool. But the thing was that it cost well over £200, even in the sale! In the end, my mum lent me half the money. I'm really pleased I got it. It'll stay in fashion for years, I'm sure.

Speaker 3 Chris: I don't buy many clothes. Until last Saturday, I had two pairs of jeans and some T-shirts and that was about it. But I saw a great pair of trousers in town, dark green and really well made. My girlfriend was with me when I tried them on. She hated them. She prefers me in jeans, you see. Anyway, I decided to get them. I bought this cap in the same colour, too. Nice, isn't it?

Pronunciation

5 **1 24** The last letters of the alphabet can get forgotten! Write them on the board – W, X, Y, Z – and elicit each one. Note that the letter Z is pronounced /zed / in British English and /zi: / in American English. Draw students' attention to the pictures, which will help them to remember the sounds /w/ as in *waiter*, /ks/ as in *taxi*, /j/ as in *yellow* and /z/ as in *zebra*. Play the recording of Speaker 1, Ben, which contains various words with *w*, *x*, and *y*. Ask students to complete the sentences and repeat what they hear.

Answers
1 work; waiter; Wednesday
2 yesterday; yellow
3 wonderful
4 extra

6 **1 25**

Recording script and answers
1 zoo
2 wool
3 young
4 excellent
5 zero
6 water
7 year
8 expensive
9 yogurt
10 women
11 exam
12 worry

Reading

7 Key Reading Part 3

In this first part of Reading Part 3, students are given two-line conversations covering functions and situations in everyday English. Suggest students try out all three options in each conversation before choosing their answers.

Answers
1 B 2 C 3 A 4 C 5 B

Activity

Explain that the activity practises the spelling of clothes vocabulary. Students in each group should take it in turns to choose the words to be spelled and check correct spelling with you or in a dictionary if necessary.

Writing folder 2

SB pages 48–49

Writing Part 7 Open cloze

Ask students to read the information about this part of the Reading and Writing paper.

1   Ask students to add more words to each set and compare examples in pairs.

Possible answers

articles:	an, the
pronouns:	me, they
prepositions:	on, in
quantifiers:	any, every
auxiliary verbs:	has, had
modal verbs:	must, should

2   Elicit answers quickly.

Answers
1   pronoun: *you*
2   auxiliary verb: *did/do*
3   preposition: *to*
4   modal verb: *should*
5   quantifier: *any*
6   article: *a*

3   Remind students that in the exam there may be two short texts, like these messages. In the exam, candidates aren't given words to choose from, but this type of guided task can be useful as exam preparation for weaker students. Using a Part 7 task from any past paper, give students two or three options for each space, including the correct answers. In this way, students will become more familiar with the task and gain enough confidence to tackle the 'open' spaces.

Answers
1   in
2   some
3   for
4   must
5   our
6   from
7   much
8   Do
9   because
10 the

Part 7

Ask students to read the Exam advice and do the task on their own. Elicit answers. Alternatively, this exam task can be done as homework.

Answers
41   some
42   me
43   There
44   for
45   because/where
46   it
47   much
48   on
49   are
50   my

8 Entertainment

8.1 A great movie	
Grammar	Modal verbs 1: *can, could, may, might, must, have to, had to*
Exam skills	Reading Part 5: Multiple-choice cloze

8.2 Cool sounds	
Vocabulary	Music and concerts
Exam skills	Listening Part 1: Short conversations
Pronunciation	Short questions
Spelling	Mistakes with vowels

8.1 A great movie

SB pages 50–51

1 Elicit the English titles of the films: the photos show stills from *Avatar, Pirates of the Caribbean (On Stronger Tides)* and *The Adventures of Tintin.*

Lead a brief class discussion on the popularity of these films, using the phrases given. If your students are not familiar with these films, ask them which of the features listed are most important in a film.

2 Students ask each other the questions about films.

Grammar

3

Answers
1 I <u>can</u> understand most films in French.
2 Jenny <u>may</u> buy that DVD, but she's not sure.
3 You <u>must</u> book in advance for the 3D film.
4 I <u>had to</u> take my passport to the cinema to show my age.
5 When he was in New York, Roberto <u>could</u> see a different movie every night.
6 Cinema staff sometimes <u>have to</u> work very long hours.
7 My brother <u>might</u> have an extra ticket for tonight's film – I'll ask him.
Note that in the present tense *have to* has a slightly different usage from *must* but, at A2 level, students needn't worry about the distinction.

4 This provides students with an explanation and example of when we use each modal verb.

Answers
a 3,6 b 4 c 2,7 d 1 e 5

5 Ask students to complete the notes and examples in pairs. Elicit answers.

Completed notes
• We cannot use the word *must* in the past. Instead, we use *had to.*
Example: *Last night, I had to do my homework.*
• When we are talking about something we are unable to do, we use the word *cannot* or the contracted form *can't.*
Example: *I can't ride a horse, but I'd like to be able to.*
• If we are talking about something we were unable to do in the past, we use *could not* or the contracted form *couldn't.*
Example: *Before I was five, I couldn't read, but now I can.*

6 Ask students to complete the exercise on their own. Elicit answers round the class.

Answers
1 can't 2 had to 3 couldn't 4 could 5 Can
6 must 7 may 8 have to

7 Ask students to complete the table and then work in groups of four or five. Encourage them to expand a little when comparing their answers, e.g. *I might go into town with a friend on Saturday and buy some clothes.*

ⓔxtension activity

Ask students to write sentences about problem visits to the cinema, to elicit *had to* and *couldn't.* Brainstorm some possible scenarios, for example they tried to see a film that was fully booked (they *couldn't* get in and *had to* go back another day); they got tickets but didn't sit where they wanted to (they *couldn't* get tickets at the back, so they *had to* sit at the front); they took someone's little brother who got bored (he *couldn't* sit quietly so we all *had to* leave), etc.

Reading

8 **Key** Reading Part 5

The photo shows a still from *Transformers 3.* This exam-level task can be set for homework if time is short.

Answers
1 B 2 B 3 C 4 A 5 B 6 A 7 C 8 C

8.2 Cool sounds

SB pages 52–53

1 Ask students to discuss their top bands and then take a class vote on the most popular band.

Vocabulary

2 Suggest students work on the word square in pairs and then use the words to describe the photo. The band in the photo is Kasabian.

Answers
play, dance, guitar, album, speakers, singer, lights, festival, drums, piano, concert, band

s	l	q	f	b	s	p	l	a	y
i	d	w	e	a	t	i	t	e	t
n	d	w	s	t	d	a	n	c	e
g	u	i	t	a	r	n	j	o	x
e	l	n	i	o	u	o	w	n	e
r	i	t	v	k	m	v	s	c	i
p	g	x	a	e	s	u	a	e	b
b	h	a	l	b	u	m	r	r	a
o	t	a	m	p	d	a	t	t	n
l	s	p	e	a	k	e	r	s	d

Possible answers
The band has a guitarist and a singer.
The guitarist is also singing.
The singer might be dancing.
We can see some drums and a big speaker.
There are lights. It looks like a concert.

Listening

3 **Key Listening Part 1**

🔊 26 These conversations are at *Key* level, but in the exam there would be a wider range of topics, rather than this single focus on music. Remind students that the questions are also recorded. You will hear each recording twice.

Answers
1 A 2 B 3 C 4 B 5 A

Recording script

1 *How much did Craig earn from the concert?*
Boy: The band earned a hundred and fifty pounds last night. That's the best yet!
Girl: But what did they pay you, Craig? You booked the concert, so you should earn more than the other two.
Boy: I don't agree. We took <u>fifty pounds</u> each and that's fine.
Girl: Well, they must give you half next time. Seventy-five pounds sounds right to me!
Now listen again.
(The recording is repeated.)

2 *Which band did the girl see?*
Girl: I saw a good band at last Saturday's rock festival. The singer was great!
Boy: The band with the piano player? He sang well, didn't he?
Girl: I didn't see anything with a piano. This singer was called Queen Cat. She could really dance too.
Boy: Oh, I know who you mean – <u>the band had three guitars</u>. Yes, excellent.
Now listen again.
(The recording is repeated.)

3 *Where is the next band from?*
Boy: Who's on next, Kate? Is it that Brazilian band? They're great!
Girl: Yeah, they are, but they're not on until this evening. It's a new <u>band from Iceland now</u> … you know, where the singer Bjork is from.
Boy: Sounds interesting. I enjoyed that last band from Australia. Did you?
Girl: No, they were boring.
Now listen again.
(The recording is repeated.)

4 *What does Ben play?*
Boy: Hi, Anna. Tell me, is your brother <u>Ben still playing the drums</u>? We want someone tonight because Ray's ill.
Girl: Is he? Ben still plays, but he's away this week. I'm learning the keyboards, you know.
Boy: Great. Perhaps you can play in our band one day, then!
Girl: Can I? Ben says the guitar's a better choice because all bands have guitar players.
Now listen again.
(The recording is repeated.)

5 *What must Kim bring to the party?*
Girl: Hello, Kim. Listen, I want some special lights for my party tonight. Can you bring some?
Boy: Sorry, Tracey, I can't. Try the music shop in town. Do you want to borrow my guitar tonight?

Girl: No thanks, but <u>don't forget your new albums</u>. I'll phone the shop about the lights now.

Boy: OK. See you later.

Now listen again.

(The recording is repeated.)

Pronunciation

4   **1 27** Play the example of short questions. Explain that using short questions like Anna does is a good way of sounding more natural in English. Then pause the recording and make sure students understand what they have to do.

   1 28 Remind students to listen carefully to the verb that is used in each sentence, so they know which auxiliary verb to use in the question. Refer them back to the example with Anna if necessary.

   Play the recording, which has a short pause after each statement for students to write the sentence number next to the question.

   Then let students listen to both parts of the conversations to check their answers.

Answers
1 Did I?
2 Have you?
3 Aren't they?
4 Can't you?
5 Isn't it?
6 Did they?

Recording script
(NB The sentences are recorded twice: the first time you will hear sentences 1 to 6 with Speaker 1 only, with a pause for students to write their answers; the second time you will also hear Speaker 2, so that students can check their answers.)

1

Speaker 1: Here's your scarf. You left it at my house after the party.

(pause)

Speaker 2: Did I?

2

Speaker 1: I've got tickets for Adele's next concert.

(pause)

Speaker 2: Have you?

3

Speaker 1: Jon and Alice aren't coming to see the band now.

(pause)

Speaker 2: Aren't they?

4

Speaker 1: We went to Glastonbury last summer but we can't this year.

(pause)

Speaker 2: Can't you?

5

Speaker 1: The next band's not on until midnight.

(pause)

Speaker 2: Isn't it?

6

Speaker 1: Casio Kids played six songs from their new album.

(pause)

Speaker 2: Did they?

5   **1 29** Play the recording, this time asking students to say the short question and add a short phrase after it. Pause the recording if they need extra time.

Possible answers
1 Did I? Thanks a lot.
2 Have you? That's great! / Fantastic!
3 Aren't they? What a pity. / That's a shame.
4 Can't you? That's a shame. / What a pity.
5 Isn't it? That's too bad. / That's a shame.
6 Did they? Fantastic! / That's great!

6   The questions not used in exercise 4 are *Must I?*, *Don't you?* and *Couldn't she?* Ask students to write the conversations in pairs and then elicit answers.

Spelling spot

7   The spelling errors featured here are among the most common ones in the Cambridge Learner Corpus at Key level.

Answers
1 Yesterday I was at a *beautiful* rock concert.
2 It's my *favourite* cinema.
3 I'm selling my piano *because* I don't want it any more.
4 A lot of *tourists* visit my town.
5 I went to a nightclub with my *friends*.
6 There are two *museums* in the town.

Activity

The photo is of Jay-Z. Suggest students work on similar pictures of famous people in disguise and bring them to the next lesson. They should include some sentences about the star as clues.

Units 5–8 Revision

SB pages 54–55

This revision unit recycles the language and topics from Units 5–8, as well as providing exam practice for Reading Part 5 and Writing Part 7.

Speaking

1 Encourage students to say as much as possible about each sentence.

Grammar

2

> **Answers**
> 1 C 2 B 3 C 4 A

3

> **Answers**
> 1 B 2 C 3 A 4 B 5 C 6 C 7 B 8 A

Vocabulary

4

> **Answers**
> 1 tall
> 2 hot
> 3 dirty
> 4 boring
> 5 old
> 6 fast
> 7 thin
> 8 small (Other adjectives would be possible here, but they have all been used already.)

5 Encourage students to record new vocabulary in topic groups.

> **Answers**
> *Animals:* bear, elephant, fish, horse, lion, monkey
> *Clothes:* button, jacket, jeans, pocket, shorts, socks, sweater, trainers
> *Music:* album, concert, drums, guitar, piano
> *Activities:* chess, climbing, cycling, skateboarding, table tennis

Writing

6

> **Answers**
> 1 to
> 2 It
> 3 were
> 4 more
> 5 at/in/inside
> 6 best/greatest/coolest
> 7 because/as
> 8 his
> 9 may/might/could
> 10 why

9 Travel

9.1 Holiday plans	
Listening	Listening for specific information
Grammar	The future with *going to*
Pronunciation	/h/
Exam skills	Reading Part 3: Functional English

9.2 Looking into the future	
Vocabulary	Travel
Reading	Reading for specific information
Grammar	The future with *will*
Spelling	Words ending in *-y*
Exam skills	Writing Part 7: Cloze

Preparation

Make one copy of the *Holiday island* map on the Teacher's Audio CD/CD-ROM (Photocopiable activities, page 7) for each group of four to five students for the Extension activity in 9.1.

9.1 Holiday plans
SB pages 56–57

1 Ask students to work in pairs to discuss if any of the types of holiday in the photos appeals to them and what their idea of a perfect holiday would be.

Listening

2 **1 30** Play the recording and ask students to match the people with the places and the types of holiday. Then play it again and ask them to listen for how each person is going to travel.

Answers		
1 Julia	Australia	beach
2 Daniel	Switzerland	walking
3 Simon	France	camping
4 Natalie	Greece	sailing
5 Julia – by plane and car		
6 Daniel – by motorbike		
7 Simon – by train		
8 Natalie – by boat		

Recording script
Daniel: Hi, Julia!
Julia: Daniel! Hi, how are you?
Daniel: I'm fine. I hear you're on holiday next week – are you going to go to Florida again with your parents?

Julia: No, Australia this time. My father's friend has a flat by a beautiful beach. We're going to fly to Sydney and then drive along the coast to the flat. What about you?
Daniel: I'm going to do some walking in Switzerland with my older brother. I did ask a friend to come with me but he's decided to stay at home this year – he wants to save enough money to buy a car. We're going to go on my brother's motorbike. Oh, there's Natalie and Simon. We're just talking about holidays. Are you planning anything, Simon?
Simon: Hi! I'm going to go camping with my family again. We're catching a train down to the south of France, which will be great. Some of my friends are driving to Italy, so they're going to visit us on the way.
Daniel: What about you, Natalie?
Natalie: My cousin has asked me to go with her to Greece. We're going to hire a boat and then sail around the Greek islands for three whole weeks! I can't wait!
Daniel, Simon and Julia: That sounds really good! Wow! Amazing.

Grammar

Refer the class to the grammar explanation. Put the time line on the board and give some other examples:
Yesterday I decided to go to the cinema on (today's date).
Tonight I'm going to go to the cinema.

Check that students understand that when the verb we want to use is already *go*, then we sometimes just say, for example, *I'm going to the café at lunchtime.* This is the present continuous form, which is also used for talking about the future, but more for already completed arrangements than plans. Sometimes there is very little difference in meaning:
I'm washing my hair tonight.
I'm going to wash my hair tonight.
But there can sometimes be a small difference:
I'm having burgers and ice cream for dinner. (They're in the fridge.)
I'm going to have burgers and ice cream at the weekend. (This is the plan.)

3 Invite students to work in pairs to ask and answer questions about the pictures.

Suggested answers
2 He's going (to go) swimming / dive into the pool.
3 They're going to play tennis.
4 He's going to buy/have/eat an ice cream.
5 They're going to have a pizza.
6 She's going (to go) cycling.

4

Answers
2 is going to telephone
3 are going to do
4 am going to book
5 is going to visit
6 is/are going to close
7 are going to meet
8 are/'re going to have

Extension activity ◉

Students should form groups of four or five. Give each group one copy of the *Holiday island* map on the Teacher's Audio CD/CD-ROM (Photocopiable activities, page 7). The group is going to make a perfect holiday island. They can mark on the map any of the following:
hotels (how many is up to the group)
tennis courts
swimming pools
beaches
restaurants
clubs
a museum / historical site
the airport
shops / shopping centre
banks
golf course
plus anything else they think is necessary

After they have finished their discussion and completed the map, ask them to write a short description of the island for the Travel section of a newspaper. They could do this for homework.

Pronunciation

5 **1 31** Ask the class to underline the words in the exercise which contain the sound /h/ as in *hand*. Play the recording so they can check their answers.

Answers
The words which contain the sound /h/ are: hand, holiday, home, hill, how, happy, hotel
The words which don't include the sound /h/ are: why, when, honest, hour, school

6 **1 32** Ask the class to work in pairs to put the words in each sentence in the right order. They should then listen to the recording to check their answers.

Recording script and answers
1 He has a holiday home in the hills.
2 Helena hopes she'll get a horse for her birthday.
3 Help him with his homework.
4 Have a happy holiday!
5 I'm going to hire a boat and have fun.
6 Help me into the helicopter!

7 **1 33** Ask the class to listen to the recording and circle the word they hear in each pair.

Answers
1 high
2 hold
3 it
4 and
5 air
6 hall
7 art

Reading

8 Key Reading Part 3

This exercise gives more practice for Reading Part 3. Stella has gone to a travel agent to book a holiday. Ask students to work in pairs and discuss which of the sentences A–H would best fit in gaps 1–5. They should also discuss why the extra sentences do not fit and talk about when they could be used.

Answers
1 C 2 A 3 G 4 E 5 B

9.2 Looking into the future
SB pages 58–59

Vocabulary

1 Ask the class to match 1–10 with a–j.

Answers
1 d 2 j 3 b 4 a 5 h 6 f 7 i 8 c 9 e 10 g

2 Ask the students to work in pairs or groups to discuss 1–6. Check that they understand *will/won't* and can pronounce them correctly.

Reading

3   The students should read through the text and then look at the question prompts and answers 1–7. Check that they understand the example and what they have to do. There might be a number of variations permissible.

Suggested answers
2 Where will we/people have holidays?
3 How will we/people travel?
4 Where will the mirrors be?
5 What will the mirrors tell you?
6 Why won't there be (any) curtains? / Why will there be no curtains?
7 Where will the food come from?

Grammar

Go through the examples in the grammar explanation. Make sure that the students understand the idea of 'certainly', 'probably' and 'possibly'. Ask them to give you some examples of their own and put them up on the board.

4   Ask a couple of members of the class to say a sentence about each of the topics. Ask the class to write some sentences for themselves on the given topics, predicting what will happen in the future, then to compare their sentences with a partner.

5   **Key Writing Part 7**

Ask the class to read through the email. Ask them:
Where is Susie staying?
How does she feel?
What is she going to do tonight?

In the exam, candidates do not have a choice of words to fill the spaces with. They are given an open cloze, that is, a text with ten spaces which they have to fill. The exercise here is to get students used to dealing with a cloze.

Answers
1 on
2 a
3 going
4 is
5 but
6 its
7 can
8 there
9 some
10 will

ⒺExtension activity

Ask students each to write a Facebook message to a friend from a holiday destination which they don't name. Walk round the class introducing vocabulary as necessary. When they have finished writing, ask a few students to read out what they have written and the class have to guess where each student has been on holiday.
Example:
I'm having a lovely time here. It is very hot and tomorrow I'm going to a famous theme park where there are dolphins and rollercoasters and also film studios. The beaches are wonderful! We went to see some alligators yesterday.
Love
Answer: Florida – Disneyworld at Orlando

Spelling spot

6   Read through the explanation and check that everyone understands. Ask the class to work through the exercise.

Answers
2 plays
3 happier
4 key(s)
5 monkeys
6 batteries
7 enjoyed
8 stays
9 families
10 buys

Activity

Explain that the class should look at the questionnaire on page 132 of their Student's Book. Ask them to predict what kind of traveller they will be: *World Traveller, Happy Tourist* or *Stay-at-Home*.

Invite them to do the questionnaire with a partner. They take turns to ask their partner the questions and make a note of their answers. They then look at the scores on page 134 and tell their partner the result.

Exam folder 5

SB pages 60–61

Speaking Parts 1 and 2

Part 1

1 **1 34** Play the recording and explain that the class will hear an interview which will include the type of questions that are asked in the exam.

Explain that in Part 1, after an initial greetings phase, students respond to specific questions about themselves. Part 1 develops to test a range of tenses and elicit a more extended response by the candidate, with a broader instruction given by the examiner, for example *Tell me something about your hobbies.* Students can show their range of language here.

Answers
Name: Pilar Martinez
Town/country: Madrid, Spain
Favourite subject: English
Countries visited: England, France, Portugal
Free-time activities: shopping, going out with friends, cinema

Recording script
Examiner: Good morning.
Candidate: Good morning.
Examiner: What's your name?
Candidate: My name is Pilar Martinez.
Examiner: How do you spell your surname?
Candidate: It's M-A-R-T-I-N-E-Z.
Examiner: And where do you come from?
Candidate: I come from Madrid, in Spain.
Examiner: Where do you study?
Candidate: I study at a school here in Madrid.
Examiner: And which subjects do you study?
Candidate: I ... I study English... and History and Geography.
Examiner: Which subject do you like best?
Candidate: Oh ... English, of course!
Examiner: Why do you like it?
Candidate: Mmm ... I enjoy learning languages, and I think ... I need English – you know, for a job later.
Examiner: Have you ever been to other countries?
Candidate: Yes, as well as England, I have been to France.
Examiner: What are you going to do next weekend?

Candidate: Next weekend it's ... it's my friend's birthday and she is having a big party.
Examiner: Tell me something about what you do in your free time.
Candidate: Erm ... In my free time I play tennis. I like tennis because it keeps me fit. I feel great! Um, I also go shopping, I ... I like doing that with my friends and ... and I go to the cinema.
Examiner: Thank you.

2 Invite the students to work in pairs.

3 Encourage students to keep talking about the topic. They should try to produce longer sentences in this phase of Part 1, using conjunctions such as *because, but, so.*

Part 2

4

Holiday Centre – possible questions and answers
B: Where is it?
A: It's in/at Westcliffe on Sea.
B: What can I do there?
A: You can go swimming and play tennis.
B: How much is it for an adult? / How much does it cost for an adult? / What's the price for an adult?
A: It's £400 for a week in July.
B: Is it open all year?
A: No, only from March to November
B: Is there a place to eat? / Can I eat there?
A: Yes, there's an excellent restaurant.

5 The candidates change roles, with B having the information and A asking the questions.

Burford Arts Cinema – possible questions and answers
A: What can I see at the cinema?
B: You can see/watch an adventure film. / You can see *The Return of the Martians.*
A: What time does the film start? / When does the film start?
B: It starts at two o'clock.
A: Can I eat there?
B: Yes, you can eat at the Riverside Café.
A: What is the address? / Where is it?
B: It's 68 Helman Street, Burford.
A: How much is a student ticket? / How much does a student ticket cost?
B: It's £5.00.

10 Places and buildings

10.1 Inside the home	
Vocabulary	Furniture; rooms; colours; materials; Adjectives – opposites
Spelling	Words ending in *-f* and *-fe*
Exam skills	Listening Part 2: Matching Reading Part 2: Lexical multiple choice

10.2 Famous buildings	
Pronunciation	Dates in years
Grammar	The passive – present and past simple

Preparation

For the Activity in 10.2, make copies of the cards on the Teacher's Audio CD/CD-ROM (Photocopiable activities, page 8) and cut them up so that there are enough cards for each pair of students to have about 10 cards.

10.1 Inside the home
SB pages 62–63

Vocabulary

1 Ask students to look at the picture of a teenager's bedroom and match the vocabulary items with the pictures a–o.

Answers
1 d 2 j 3 g 4 l 5 m 6 i 7 n 8 o 9 k
10 c 11 h 12 b 13 e 14 f 15 a

2 Ask the class to work in pairs. They should talk about their own rooms at home. They should refer to the colours in the book and use the language from the speech bubbles.

Spelling spot

3

Answers
2 I have *some bookshelves* in my room.
3 *The knives are* on the table.
4 *The roofs are* red.
5 *Their wives are* in the kitchen.
6 I found *some leaves* on the floor.

Listening

4 Ask students to look at the objects 1–6 in their books and the names of the rooms. They should talk with a partner about which room they would expect to find the objects in. For example, in their house or flat do they have a mirror in the bedroom or the bathroom, or maybe in both?

5 **Key Listening Part 2**

🔊 35 In Part 2 of the Listening paper candidates must listen to identify key information. They hear an informal conversation and have to match five items with a choice of eight items.

Ask the class to read through the exercise and check they understand the vocabulary and what they have to do.

Answers
1 D 2 F 3 H 4 A 5 B

Recording script
Lisa: Hi, Tom!
Tom: Oh hi, Lisa! How's the new flat?
Lisa: It's great! But we haven't finished moving all our furniture yet. The <u>metal desk</u> from my old room <u>is still in the garage</u> with lots of other things!
Tom: Did you have any problems when you moved?
Lisa: A few. The <u>leather sofa</u> was too big for the living room so <u>it's in the dining room</u> for now.
Tom: What's your new <u>bedroom</u> like?
Lisa: It's bigger than my old one and I can have the <u>computer in there</u> now. We had it in the corner of the kitchen before. My parents have put the <u>small TV in their room</u>, but they said I could have one for my birthday!
Tom: Great! What about that large <u>mirror</u> you had in the kitchen? Have you still got it?
Lisa: Yes, and it looks really good <u>in the new bathroom</u>. And do you remember my mum's books? Well, she now has <u>new bookshelves in the hall</u> – it's much better than the books being in their bedroom! Why don't you come and see us this evening?
Tom: That'd be great. I'll do that.

Vocabulary

6   Students can work through the pictures in pairs or as a class exercise.

Answers
the bag – leather or plastic
the book – paper
the bowl – wood
the credit card – plastic
the curtains – cotton
the necklace – gold
the sweater – wool
the TV – glass, metal and plastic
the vase – glass
the watch – silver, metal, glass
the window – glass and wood/plastic

Extension activity

Ask the class to work in pairs or small groups – possibly single sex. They should have one piece of clean A4 paper and on it they should design the perfect bedroom. They should discuss their ideas, saying, for example:
Where shall we put the bed?
We could put the TV on a shelf.
Let's put the DVD player in the corner.
After 15–20 minutes they should present their bedroom to the rest of the class.
Useful language
in the middle/corner of the room
on the wall
at the side of the room
at the top/bottom of the wall
between the door and the window
over the bed
under the table
on the table
by / next to the bed

7   Ask students to work in pairs.

Answers

big	little
cold	hot
double	single
expensive	cheap
high	low
large	small
long	short
narrow	wide
new	old
noisy	quiet
soft	hard

8   *Key* Reading Part 2

This exercise can be done in class or for homework. When they have finished, students should compare their answers with another student and discuss why the other adjectives are wrong.

Answers
1 B   2 C   3 A   4 A   5 B

Activity

Ask the students to work in pairs and talk about objects in their classroom using the adjectives from exercises 6 and 7. One student should give wrong information and the other should correct them. Look at the speech bubbles for an example.

10.2 Famous buildings
SB pages 64–65

1   Invite students to look at the photos. They should talk about which they would like to visit and then say where the buildings are and when they were built. You can ask about the designer or who built the building but don't make this an important point. Make sure they know how to pronounce the dates. (More work is done on dates in exercise 2.)

Answers
The designers and builders are just here for information – no one expects the students to know who they were.

1	Empire State Building	New York, USA	1931	designed by Tom Wright
2	Opera House	Sydney, Australia	1959–73	designed by Jørn Utzon
3	Taj Mahal	Agra, India	1653	built by Shah Jehan
4	Burj al Arab	Dubai, UAE	1999	built by the government of UAE
5	Forbidden City	Beijing, China	1420	built by the Ming Emperors
6	Great Pyramid	Cairo, Egypt	2500BC	built by King Khufu

Pronunciation

2   **1 36** Ask the class to write the dates as words. Then play the recording so they can check their answers.

3 **1 37** Students write the dates as numbers this time. Pause the recording if they need extra time.

Grammar

Go through the grammar explanation in the Student's Book with the class. Refer them also to the Grammar folder on page 143 of the Student's Book. There is an extra exercise there which they can do in class or for homework.

Explain that we use the passive when:
– we don't know who did something
– what happened is more important than who did it. If we want to say who did it we use *by* + the person's name.

For example:
My bag was stolen. (We don't know who by.)
The Taj Mahal was built by Shah Jehan. (The building is more important than the person.)

4

5 Ask students to comment on the photo of the London Eye. Has anyone been on it? What do they think it would be like? Would they like to go on it?

Ask them to work through the exercise. It might be helpful at this stage to demonstrate on the board the difference between the active and passive as this is what is tested here.

6 This exercise gives practice in making questions in the passive.

Extension activity

Ask the class to prepare a quiz for homework. Each student should prepare five questions and the answers to bring back to ask the class. There should be a mixture of dates/people/places. For example:

Neil Armstrong went to the moon in
A 1969. **B** 1956. **C** 1971.
The Pyramids were built by
A the Greeks. **B** the Egyptians. **C** the Libyans.

Activity

◎ Make copies of the Activity cards on the Teacher's Audio CD/CD-ROM. You should make enough cards for each pair of students to have about ten cards each.

Invite students to work in pairs. Give each pair a pile of cards face down. Each player takes it in turns to pick up a card and say what the two things on it have in common. They must use the passive.

a newspaper / a magazine	They are both made of paper / read by people.
biscuits / juice	They are both bought in supermarkets.
The English language / The Hindi language	They are both spoken in India.
Romeo and Juliet / Hamlet	They were both written by Shakespeare.
bananas / sugar	They are both grown in the Caribbean.
horses / bicycles	They are both ridden by people.
a tie / trousers	They are both worn by men.
football / basketball	They are both played in teams.
vegetables / clothes	They are both sold in markets.

Exam folder 6

SB pages 66–67

Reading Part 4
Right, Wrong, Doesn't say

Ask students to read the information about this part of the Reading and Writing paper. Refer them to the Exam advice. Check they understand what they have to do.

Ask the class to look at the example of the OMR answer sheet, where they need to record their answers in the exam. They should be reminded that it is very important to record the right answer on the right line as it is very easy to 'jump' a line in the exam and lose marks.

Background information

George Hearst was a rich miner and he bought 40,000 acres of land in 1865. In 1919 his only son, William Randolph Hearst, inherited the land, now nearly 250,000 acres.

1 Students need to understand that all the information they must use is in the texts. It doesn't matter what they, personally, know and so they mustn't answer any of the questions before reading the text. The three questions give practice in this. Ask them to look at questions 1–3 and then to find the answers in the text.

Answers
1 *The castle is bigger than other houses in California.*
   You might think this is true or know for a fact that it is true, but it doesn't actually say so in the text. The answer you should give according to the text is *C* Doesn't say.
2 *Hearst Castle is one very large building.*
   Usually, a castle is one large building, but if you read the text you will see that the castle is made up of four houses. The answer you should give is *B* Wrong.
3 *Very famous American singers went to parties at Hearst Castle.*
   You would imagine this to be true. However, the text only says 'Hollywood film stars' often came to the parties. It doesn't mention singers. The answer you should give is *C* Doesn't say.

Part 4

The class should read through the text again and look carefully at the examples 0, 00 and 000. There is only one example in the actual exam.

Ask the class to work through the text and do the exam task. The questions are in the order in which the answers occur in the text.

Answers
21 B 22 B 23 A 24 C 25 A 26 C 27 B

11.1 Living for sport	
Vocabulary	Sports and sports equipment
Listening	Identifying gist meaning
Pronunciation	/b/ and /v/
Exam skills	Reading Part 4: three-option multiple-choice questions
Grammar extra	Word order in questions

11.2 Keeping fit	
Grammar	Verbs in the -ing form
Exam skills	Listening Part 5: Gap-fill
	Writing Part 6: Spelling
Spelling	gu- , qu-

Preparation

Make a copy of the recording script on the Teacher's Audio CD/CD-ROM (Photocopiable activities, page 9) for each student. This will be used in 11.2.

11.1 Living for sport

SB pages 68–69

Vocabulary

1 Refer students to the photos and ask them to discuss the questions in pairs or small groups for two minutes. Then elicit their ideas.

2 Suggest that students make lists for each sport.

Answers
surfing: board
tennis: ball, court, net, racket
baseball: ball, bat, boots, glove
basketball: ball, basket, boots, court, net, stadium
snowboarding: board, boots, gloves
volleyball: ball, court, net

3 **2 02** Explain that it is not important for students to understand every word in these recordings. Play each recording twice if necessary.

Answers

	sport	play/do or watch?
Speaker 1	tennis	play
Speaker 2	basketball	watch
Speaker 3	baseball	watch
Speaker 4	snowboarding	do
Speaker 5	surfing	do
Speaker 6	volleyball	watch

Recording script

Speaker 1: I'm doing really well this year. I bought a new racket, perhaps that's why! The main thing is I can hit the ball much harder now. I've won my last three matches.

Speaker 2: They have matches on television here every week and I sometimes go to support the college team. Last time I went, they scored twenty-nine baskets, but they still lost!

Speaker 3: Last year, I stayed in New York with my uncle and he got tickets for the Yankees. I loved every minute of the game, it was so exciting. He gave me a bat to bring home. I haven't used it. It's on my bedroom shelf!

Speaker 4: It's much more fun than skiing. I tried it for the first time last month, when the snow was very good. I'm saving for my own board now. There are some awesome videos on the Internet – I want to be as good as those guys!

Speaker 5: I had a week of lessons in Portugal. The sea was very warm there. Back in England, I have to wear a wetsuit because it's very cold and I spend a lot of time in the water!

Speaker 6: My friends and I usually go to the beach for the Saturday matches because we're big fans of one of the women's teams there. It's a really exciting game and those girls can run and jump! They're amazing.

Pronunciation

4 **2 03** The focus is on the sounds /b/ as in *basketball* and /v/ as in *volleyball*. Draw students' attention to the pictures. Explain that it is important to pronounce these two consonants clearly, to make them sound different from each other. Play the recording twice if necessary.

5 Give students the beginning of a sentence if they have difficulty getting started. For example, *Before breakfast, I visited a very beautiful ...*

Reading

6 *Key* Reading Part 4

This is a training exercise, looking at three-option multiple-choice questions. Ask students to read each question carefully and then choose the correct response.

Answers
1 B 2 C 3 A 4 C 5 B 6 A

Background information

Eniola Aluko began training for the England women's team at 14. She was a member of the Great Britain squad at the 2012 London Olympics.

7 Suggest students each write up to five short sentences on their own. Then write some of these on the board.

Possible answers
She's got a brother.
She plays football in different American cities.
She prefers playing in the USA. (11.2 focuses on the gerund/-*ing* form)
She often eats pasta before a match.
She doesn't play in goal.

Following the work on question forms in Units 1 and 2, this reminds students about word order in questions, which the *Cambridge Learner Corpus* has shown to be a problem for *Key* candidates. Ask students to read the information carefully before doing the exercise.

8

Grammar e*x*tra

Answers
2 Which team does Lionel Messi play for?
3 Have you got a snowboard?
4 When is the next World Cup?
5 Why didn't you go to the match?
6 Which is your favourite sport? / Which sport is your favourite?
7 Where does the referee come from?
8 Do you want to swim in the competition?

9 Remind students that in Part 2 of the Speaking test they will have to form questions from a card like this one.

Possible questions
When is the sports competition?
Which sports will there be?
Will the sports competition be at the college or somewhere else?
What clothes should I wear?
Are there any prizes in the competition?

11.2 Keeping fit

SB pages 70–71

1 Give students two or three minutes to discuss their views. Elicit their ideas.

2 This flow chart is taken from a British teenage magazine. Suggest students work through it in pairs.

Grammar

3 Elicit all the examples – there are ten more in all.

Answers
spend more time <u>playing</u> computer games
<u>going</u> out with your friends
<u>winning</u>
keep <u>taking</u> the lift
<u>walking</u> to school
<u>relaxing</u>
<u>exercising</u>
<u>sleeping</u> in a maths lesson
start <u>playing</u> some sport
stop <u>exercising</u>

4

Answers
1 sitting	4 getting	7 running
2 making	5 driving	8 throwing
3 swimming	6 playing	9 carrying

5 Ask students to complete the exercise and then compare answers.

Answers
2 hitting
3 going
4 moving
5 walking
6 winning
7 playing; scoring
8 practising

6 Encourage students to use *really*, to sound more natural. Give them a couple of minutes to talk about 1–8 in pairs. Then elicit answers round the class.

Extension activity

Ask students to prepare a class poster covering some of their favourite (and least favourite) activities. Encourage students to bring in photos of themselves doing these activities. They should write sentences to go with the photos using -*ing* forms. For example, *Paola really loves playing beach volleyball*.

Listening

7

2 **04** Remind students to check their spelling carefully. Play the recording twice.

Photocopiable recording script activity ⊙

Make copies of the recording script from the Teacher's Audio CD/CD-ROM (Photocopiable activities, page 9) and hand them out after the first listening. Ask students to read it as they listen again. They can then check their own answers from the script.

Answers
1 11.15 (pm) / quarter past eleven
2 88679
3 25 / twenty-five
4 Colville
5 Tuesday

Recording script

This is the 24-hour information line for the Solway Sports Centre. Our opening hours are from six thirty in the morning until <u>eleven fifteen</u> at night, seven days a week.

If you love exercising, you'll love our gym! It has all the latest equipment. To book an introduction to the gym, please phone Jack Bergman on 01453 <u>88679</u> now.

There are two pools at the club. We have a ten-metre pool just for diving and a <u>twenty-five</u> metre swimming pool. Why not try relaxing in our steam room before you swim? It's fantastic!

If you'd like to become a member of Solway Sports Centre, please phone us again during working hours and ask to speak to Mrs <u>Colville</u>, that's C-O-L-V-I-double L-E.

We also give guided tours of the centre once a week. These tours are at two fifteen every <u>Tuesday</u> afternoon. You don't have to book a place, but don't be late!

We hope you enjoy getting fit at Solway Sports Centre!

Spelling sp⊙t

The *Cambridge Learner Corpus* shows that students sometimes omit the *u*, especially after *g*.

8

Answers
1 quickly
2 quarter
3 guitar
4 guest
5 quiet
6 guess

9

All the words in this Part 6 task are *-ing* forms.

Answers
1 skiing
2 cycling
3 fishing
4 climbing
5 sailing

Activity

This activity offers further practice of *-ing* forms. Before students start, get them to discuss as a class how to organise the survey. For example, different groups could find out the answer to each of the four questions. Make sure students spend enough time planning the survey and preparing the questions.

Writing folder 3

Writing Part 9
Short message

There are two kinds of Part 9 task: 'with input' and 'instructions only'. This Writing folder covers the 'with input' and Writing folder 5 covers the 'instructions only' type.

Ask students to read the information about this part of the Reading and Writing paper. Explain that it is very important for them to include *all three* pieces of information in their answer.

1   These exam answers have been taken from the *Cambridge Learner Corpus*. Ask students to correct the answers in pairs, following the instructions in the bulleted points.

> **Corrected answers**
> **1**
> I'm going to visit your town next Friday. I'd like to visit the sports club near your house. I think it's a very nice place. Meet me at 7 p.m.
> Yours,
>
> **2**
> I think that the most interesting place near my town is a little lake, because it's not noisy there and there are a lot of animals. You can drive to it.
> Love,
>
> **3**
> Let's meet in front of the football ground at 17.00. I want to buy a camera and a computer game. See you on Saturday.
>
> **4**
> Hello,
> I have a basketball, a football, a computer and a television to sell. The basketball and football are almost new. I've only played with them once. I've had the computer and television for six months but I want to sell them.
> Bye,

2   Elicit an answer quickly: all four answers need to be signed (see introduction).

3   Ask students to decide on the three pieces of information in pairs.

> **Answers**
> 1   information about the pool
> 2   how to get there
> 3   the best time to swim

4   Elicit answers to the three questions students were asked to think about before asking students to decide on the better answer.

> **Answer**
> Answer B is better, because it is the right length and includes all the necessary information.
> At only 20 words, answer A would lose one mark out of five. It also fails to include information about how to get to the pool from the town centre, so would only score three out of five.

5   Elicit ideas on the information that is needed and then ask students to rewrite answer A, including their ideas.

> **Possible answer**
> Hi Alex,
> There's a swimming pool near the motorway. It's really big and has a nice café, too. Why not go at lunchtime or on Saturday? You can take tram 14 from the town centre. It stops outside the pool.
> See you,
> Mario

6   Ask students to do the exercise in pairs.

> **Answers**
> B 1   C 2   D 3   E 1   F 1   G 3   H 2

7   Encourage students to use their own words and different ideas in their answers. They can do this for homework.

> **Sample answer**
> Dear Alex,
> Our pool is lovely! It's big and very deep at one end. Why not go in the afternoon, when it's not as busy? You can catch a bus or walk there. It's not too far. Have fun!
> Love,
> Ellie

12 The family

12.1 Family tree

SB pages 74–75

Background information

Scarlett Johansson has starred in some very successful films, including *The Girl with a Pearl Earring*, *Vicky Cristina Barcelona* and *Iron Man 2*.

Vocabulary

1 Ask if students have seen any of Scarlett Johansson's films. Suggest they spend two minutes reading the text and completing her family tree.

Answers
1 grandfather 2 father 3 mother
4 (older) brother 5 sister

2

Answers
1 uncle 2 aunt 3 cousin 4 grandmother
5 grandson 6 granddaughter 7 grandchild

3 Ask students to make a simple family tree, similar to the one in exercise 1. They should write in the names of their family members and their relationship to them, for example *father, brother*.

Listening

4 **Key Listening Part 3**

2 05 Play the recording twice and then elicit answers.

Answers
1 C 2 B 3 C 4 A 5 B

Recording script
Nick: Hello, Nick speaking.
Helen: Hi, it's your cousin, Helen.
Nick: How are you?
Helen: Fine. I'm ringing about Granddad's 70th birthday party. Will it be on Friday 26th, or Saturday 27th September?
Nick: Actually, Mum and Uncle Jack decided on Sunday 28th because several people couldn't do Friday or Saturday.
Helen: OK. Are you going to have the party at your house?
Nick: It's too small! There's a nice room at his golf club, so we'll have it there. There's lunch before the party, at Mario's restaurant.
Helen: Great. Will the party still start at three thirty?
Nick: No, four. We'll finish eating around two forty-five and it's an hour's drive.
Helen: Mm. I can take you there in my car.
Nick: Thanks, but I'll have mine. Why don't you take Aunt Rose, Uncle Jack's sister from Australia?
Helen: Fine. Now, what about presents? My brother's going to buy Granddad a box set of three DVDs, and there's a beautiful mirror I'd like to get for him. What do you think?
Nick: Sounds excellent. I've bought him a leather suitcase.
Helen: He'll love that. Well, see you on the day then, Nick.
Nick: Yes. Bye, Helen.

Pronunciation

5 **2 06** The focus is on the sounds /aʊ/ as in *cow* and /ɔː/ as in *draw*. Draw students' attention to the pictures. These sounds are often confused and the words misspelled.

Ask students to write the words from the box in either group 1 or group 2. Then play the recording for them to check if they were right. Play it again and ask them to repeat the words.

Spelling spot

6   Ask students to do the exercise on their own and then compare answers.

Answers
1 castle   2 bicycle   3 apple
4 single   5 little   6 people

Grammar extra

7   Check whether students already know these possessive adjectives and pronouns, which they should use in the speaking practice when talking about their family trees.

8   This will revise topic vocabulary from earlier units, as well as using some possessive pronouns. Ask two students to demonstrate the guessing game, following the examples given. Student A looks at the word lists for Units 3 and 5 on pages 149–150 (Food and drink, Animals) and Student B looks at Units 7, 10 and 11 (Clothes, The home, Sports) on pages 150–151.

Extension activity

To give further practice in possessive pronouns, do a spoken 'chain' activity round the class, like this one:
– Is this Jack's scarf?
– No, it isn't his, it's Tessa's.
– Is this Tessa's lunch?
– No, it isn't hers, it's Sam and Janet's.
– (It isn't theirs, it's mine. etc)

12.2 Large and small

SB pages 76–77

1   Ask students to discuss their views and then elicit answers. The picture shows the Hayden family, featured in the Reading section that follows. There are seven children in this family.

2   This provides further practice of *-ing* forms.

Possible answers
being by yourself   having a low supermarket bill
keeping the place tidy   travelling cheaply

Reading

3   Key Reading Part 4

Suggest students underline the relevant words.

Answer
Sam is close to Michael. (*get on quite well ... because he is kind and helps me*)

4   Ask students to skim the text to find out who Joe gets on well with.

Answer
Joe gets on well with Michael and David.

5   Remind students that if there is no information in the text, they will need to choose C, 'Doesn't say'. When eliciting answers, ask students to look at the relevant parts of the text, especially for the C answers, 3, 5 and 7.

Answers
2 B   3 C   4 B   5 C   6 A   7 C

Extension activity

Ask the class for their views on Naomi Hayden's position as the youngest in the family and the only girl. Then ask them to write a paragraph about Naomi, based on what they have just discussed.

Grammar

6   Refer students to the examples from Sam and Joe's texts and explain the differences between the three types of personal pronoun. Then ask students to complete the table.

Answers

subject pronouns	object pronouns	reflexive pronouns
I	me	myself
you	you	yourself
he, she, it	him, her, it	himself, herself, itself
we	us	ourselves
you	you	yourselves
they	them	themselves

7   Ask students to complete the sentences on their own, choosing suitable pronouns from their completed table. They can compare their answers when they have finished.

Answers
2 myself   3 them   4 himself   5 It   6 herself
7 themselves

8 Explain that *everybody* has exactly the same meaning
   as *everyone*, and similarly *anybody – anyone* and
   nobody – no one.

Answers

things	*people*
something	somebody / someone
anything	anybody / anyone
everything	everybody / everyone
nothing	nobody / no one

9 This exercise can be set for homework if time is short.

Answers

2 Somebody/Someone
3 anything
4 something
5 nobody/no one
6 everything
7 everybody/everyone
8 anybody/anyone

Activity

Suggest students form groups of four or five to discuss how
to spend the day.

Extension activity

Elicit the difference between *who* and *which* in these examples
from the texts:
My little sister, who is called Naomi, is only two.
I live in the county of Angus, which is in Scotland.

Explain that students need to understand the difference
between these relative pronouns (*who* for people and *which*
for things) as they may meet them in the Reading or Listening
components of the exam.

Write these sentences on the board and elicit answers.
1 Jonny, ... is from New Zealand, has two brothers.
2 I go dancing every week, ... I really enjoy.
3 The party, ... will start at nine o'clock, is for my
   cousin's birthday.
4 My grandfather, ... worked in Argentina, spoke
   Spanish and Italian.

Answers
1 who
2 which
3 which
4 who

Units 9–12 Revision

SB pages 78–79

This revision unit recycles the language and topics from Units 9–12, as well as providing exam practice for Reading Part 2 and training for Writing Part 9.

Speaking

1 Ask students to work on their own matching the questions and replies. Elicit answers. Then ask students to work in pairs, taking it in turn to answer the questions. Encourage them to use their own ideas and give full answers.

Answers
1 G   2 E   3 H   4 F   5 C   6 D   7 B   8 A

Grammar

2

Answers
1 I enjoyed *seeing* your family.
2 I will wait for you at the station.
3 This is the best book for *learning* English.
4 I think *it* will cost £30.
5 You don't need to ask *anybody*.
6 I don't mind *getting* the bus to your place.
7 We can ride horses and we can *fish / go fishing* in the lake.
8 If anybody *is* interested, call this number.
9 You can *come* to London by train.
10 The village is famous because it *was* built *by* three Roman emperors.

3

Answers
2 was taken   3 was shown   4 was worn
5 was written   6 is known   7 was given   8 was built

Vocabulary

4

Answers
1 racket   2 net   3 gloves   4 bat   5 snowboard

5 Explain that there may be more than one answer, depending on students' ideas.

Possible answers
1 cousin (because a cousin could be male or female)
2 desk (because everything else can go on the wall)
3 curtains (because the other three are items of furniture)
4 grey (because it has no red in it)
5 golf (because it is not played on the water)
6 silver (because it is not a kind of material, but an example of a metal)

6

Possible answers
1 C   2 B   3 B   4 A   5 B

Writing

7 Ask students to correct the punctuation and compare answers. Then ask them to decide which three questions go with each answer.

Corrected emails
A
I'd love to come sailing with you and your family, Andrea. I go sailing about ten times a year, so I've got something to wear. Can I borrow a life jacket?
B
You asked me about my room. Well, it's quite big, with two windows. From one, I can only see the street, but from the other, there's a lovely park with trees. I want some new curtains for my room.
C
I'm going to Sicily with my brother at Easter. We're going to spend a week by the sea and then we'll go walking near Etna. It's beautiful there.

Questions
Email A answers questions 3, 8 and 10.
Email B answers questions 1, 6 and 9.
Email C answers questions 2, 5 and 7.
Question 4 does not match any of the emails.

13.1 Sun, rain or snow?	
Vocabulary	Weather
Exam skills	Listening Part 2: Multiple matching
Grammar extra	*(not) as … as*
Pronunciation	unstressed words with /ə/

13.2 Weather problems	
Grammar	*enough* and *too*
Exam skills	Reading Part 5: Multiple-choice cloze
Spelling	*to, too* and *two*

Preparation

Make copies of the recording script on the Teacher's Audio CD/CD-ROM (Photocopiable activities, page 10) for each student. This will be used in 13.1.

13.1 Sun, rain or snow?
SB pages 80–81

Vocabulary

1 Invite the class to look at the photos of different types of weather. Ask them to name them: (1) *fog*, (2) *cloud*, (3) *thunderstorm/storm*, (4) *sun*, (5) *snow*, (6) *wind*, (7) *rain* and put them up on the board. They should also be familiar with the adjectives *windy, sunny, cloudy, stormy* and *foggy*.

Point out that when describing today's weather, if it is actually raining we usually say *It's raining* rather than *It's rainy*. *Rainy* is used to describe a period of time when it rains often. *Snowy* and *It's snowing* are also used in that way. Also introduce the idea of *wet* and *dry*. For example: *It's dry and sunny. It's cold and wet.*

2 The class should find the words in the word square individually, complete the sentences and then compare answers.

Answers
1 windy 2 raining 3 sunny 4 cloudy 5 wet
6 foggy 7 storms 8 dry 9 snow

3 In pairs, students should talk about the weather where they live. This may lead into a discussion about the hottest/coldest/driest places in the world.

Background information

Hottest place in the world – Death Valley, California, USA: average maximum temperature for July, 46°C.
Coldest place in the world – Polyus Nedostupnosti, Antarctica: annual mean temperature –58°C.
Wettest place in the world – Mawsynram, India: average annual rainfall 11,873 mm.
Windiest place in the world – Mount Washington, USA: wind speed of 371.75 km / hour recorded in 1934.
Probably Antarctica is the most consistently cold and windy place in the world.

4 Ask students to look at the map and discuss the weather for summer and winter in the places marked.

Listening

5 **Key** Listening Part 2

2 07 Ask students to look at the task. There is an example to help them. Play the recording twice.

Answers
1 A 2 H 3 F 4 G 5 B

Recording script
Girl: How was your trip, Dan? I'd love to go round the world.
Dan: It was great. First we went to London, but only for a few days as it rained all the time. Both of us got really wet.
Girl: You went to Paris next, didn't you?
Dan: Well, Paris wasn't at all sunny but it was better than London – a bit cloudy.
Girl: Did you go up the Eiffel Tower?
Dan: Yes, we both had a great time!
Girl: Where did you go after Paris?
Dan: To Cairo. We saw the Pyramids.
Girl: Was it very hot?
Dan: It wasn't as hot as in summer. It was quite windy, actually.
Girl: I'd love to go there.
Dan: Yes, you'd like it. We went to Sydney next. We didn't get to the famous Bondi Beach as there were a lot of storms. We did lots of shopping there.
Girl: That sounds expensive!
Dan: It wasn't as expensive as Tokyo. It was hot and sunny there – no rain at all for the whole five days we were there!

Girl: And then you went to the USA, didn't you?

Dan: Yes, to <u>San Francisco,</u> which is famous for its <u>fog.</u> It was so thick we couldn't even see the Golden Gate Bridge! But it was warmer than some of the other places!

Ⓟhotocopiable recording script activity ◉

Make copies of the recording script from the Teacher's Audio CD/CD-ROM (Photocopiable activities, page 10) and hand them out after the first listening. Play the recording again and ask students to underline where each answer comes. They can then check their own answers from the script.

Grammar eXtra

6 Refer students to the information on *(not) as ... as* etc. in their books.
Ask them to talk about the weather in the different places in the chart.

Possible answers
The weather in Beijing was cloudy yesterday, the same as in Rome.
Vancouver was not as cold as Moscow.
Mexico City was hotter than Sydney.
Athens was as warm as Madrid.

Ask the class to write six similar sentences each, either in class or for homework.

Answers
c Cairo is hotter in summer.
a Tokyo was more expensive than Sydney.

Pronunciation

7 **2 08** Ask the class to work through the exercise in pairs, filling in the missing words. When they have finished, play the recording and ask them to say what the missing words all have in common.

Recording script and answers
1 You went *to* Paris.
2 Paris was *a* bit cloudy.
3 We had *a* great time.
4 I'd love *to* go there.
5 We stayed in *a* hotel.
6 We did *some* shopping there.
7 There was no rain *at* all.
8 It was warmer *than* some of the other places.
The missing words are all unstressed, weak forms with the sound /ə/.

8 **2 09** In pairs the class should read through the sentences and underline the unstressed words which have the schwa sound /ə/.

Play the recording so students can check their answers.

Answers
1 Bob went camping with <u>a</u> friend.
2 Both <u>of</u> them like camping.
3 They got <u>to the</u> campsite late.
4 They slept <u>for</u> ten hours.
5 There <u>was</u> a good view <u>from</u> their tent.
6 They had hot chocolate <u>to</u> drink.
7 Bob took <u>some</u> great photos.

13.2 Weather problems
SB pages 82–83

1

Answers
1 True
2 True
3 False – The Atacama Desert has an average rainfall of 0.5 mm, although there are some parts of it where rainfall hasn't been recorded for 400 years!
4 True

Grammar

Refer students to the grammar explanation.

2 Ask the class to work in pairs and to look at the pictures and decide what each person is saying.

Suggested answers
1 It's too cold to go swimming. / It isn't warm enough to go swimming.
2 It's too windy to use an umbrella.
3 It's too difficult to do.
4 It's too far to walk. / I'm too tired.
5 It's too expensive to buy. / I'm not rich enough to buy it.
6 It's too heavy to carry very far. / I'm not strong enough to carry it very far.

3 Students should match one adjective with a verb to complete a sentence. Some adjectives can be used more than once.

Possible answers
2 It wasn't hot enough to lie on the beach, so we went to the cinema.
3 It was too foggy to see the road in front of the car.
4 It's too cloudy/foggy to see any stars in the sky tonight.
5 It isn't cold enough to switch on the heating in the evenings.
6 It's too windy to wear a hat – it will blow away.
7 My grandmother thought it was too icy to walk to the shops. She could easily fall.

Extension activity

Students should work in pairs.

Student A should write ten questions to ask Student B about a holiday he or she has been on.

Student B should write ten questions to ask Student A about a party he or she has been to.

Students take turns to answer each others' questions, trying to use *too* and *enough*.

Example questions and answers
A: What was the food like?
B: Terrible – it was too spicy / it wasn't hot enough.
A: What was the hotel like?
B: Awful – it was too far to walk to from the beach / it wasn't near enough to the beach.
B: What was the party like?
A: Terrible – there were too many people.
B: What was the music like?
A: Awful – it was too loud.
  Other situations could be:
  a trip to the cinema
  a day at school
  a shopping trip

Reading

4   *Key* Reading Part 5

The article is about a 'storm chaser' – a person in the USA who spends his/her time following storms, mainly to get photos but also often for research. Ask students to read through the text first to get an idea of what it is about. They should then look at the options and choose the best one.

Answers
1 B 2 B 3 A 4 B 5 C 6 B 7 A 8 C

5 Check that students understand the differences between *to*, *too* and *two*. Ask them to give you some example sentences, e.g.
   to – *I'm going to school / to do my homework.*
   too – *It's too hot to work today. I'm going home too.*
   two – *Two ice creams, please.*
   Ask them to work through the exercise.

Answers
1 I went *to* Tokyo last year for *two* weeks.
2 My cousin went *too.*
3 We took taxis *to* places because it was *too* difficult for us *to* use the subway.
4 When I got home I tried *to* cook some Japanese food.
5 I made some sushi and invited *two* friends for a meal.
6 They wanted *to* know how *to* make it so they could cook it *too.*

6

Answers
1 The weather *is* very sunny.
2 This year the weather *is* colder than last year.
3 What *is* the weather like in Australia?
4 The weather in Caracas is hotter *than* in Santiago.
5 It was not *hot enough* to go swimming.
6 I like sunny weather *very* much.

Activity

The class should form four teams – one for each season.

They should take it in turns to say a sentence about their season. For example:
In the winter I go skiing with my family.
My birthday is in winter and I get lots of presents.
Summer isn't as nice as winter because it is too hot for me.

Each correct sentence scores a point.

When the game is finished, ask students to write a paragraph about their favourite season and say why they don't like the other seasons as much.

Exam folder 7

SB pages 84–85

Listening Part 2
Multiple matching

Ask students to read the information about this part of the Listening paper.

1 This exercise practises the types of words that are tested in Part 2. Ask students to write as many words as they can in the topic sets, and give each set a title.

Possible answers

2 *Months of the year*: January, February, March, April, May, June, July, August, September, October, November, December.

3 *Sports*: football, swimming, rugby, baseball, basketball, volleyball, tennis, golf, hockey, skiing, skating, surfing, snowboarding, table tennis, skateboarding

4 *Colours*: blue, red, green, yellow, purple, pink, black, brown, white, orange, grey

5 *Clothes*: dress, jacket, trousers, jeans, blouse, T-shirt, pants, socks, coat, skirt, shorts, jumper, sweater

6 *Family*: aunt, sister, uncle, cousin, grandmother, grandfather, daughter, niece, nephew, son, father, mother

7 *Food*: apple, soup, burger, bread, salad, fish, chicken, cheese, rice, spaghetti, tomato, toast, chips

---

2 The first part of the exam task is reproduced so that students can see how the distraction works. It is important for them to realise that there are always distractors, so they don't just write down the first word they hear. They should also listen out for paraphrase.

Part 2

2 10 Refer the class to the Exam advice, and the example of the answer sheet, then play the recording and ask students to do the exam task.

Answers
6 A   7 G   8 B   9 F   10 C

Recording script

Listen to Penny talking to her cousin about the presents she bought on holiday for her friends. Which friend got each present? For questions 6 to 10 write a letter, A to H, next to each friend. You will hear the conversation twice.

Penny: Hi, Nick.

Nick: Hi, Penny. How was your holiday in Switzerland?

Penny: It was great – hot and sunny every day and some nice shops! Look, Nick, I bought you a mug. See, it's got 'Switzerland' written on it.

Nick: Oh thanks! Did you get James a pen? He's always taking mine.

Penny: I got him an album of a local band – he likes anything to do with music.

Nick: True. What about Becky? Did you get her a watch? It might help her to be on time!

Penny: She's actually getting one for her birthday, so I got her some nice soap – look, it's in a really lovely box.

Nick: Mm. She'll like that.

Penny: And for Alice – well Alice is difficult to buy for, but in the end I bought her a book about skiing.

Nick: Good idea! Now, what about Tom?

Penny: He's got lots of books about Switzerland, so I bought him a picture to put on his wall.

Nick: That leaves Lucy. You didn't get *her* a watch, did you?

Penny: No, I just got her a comb. I couldn't think of anything else.

Nick: OK. Anyway, I must go. Thanks for the mug!

Now listen again.

(The recording is repeated.)

---

14 Books and studying

<table>
<tr><td colspan="2">14.1 Something good to read</td></tr>
<tr><td>Reading</td><td>Questionnaire</td></tr>
<tr><td>Exam skills</td><td>Reading Part 4: Multiple matching</td></tr>
<tr><td>Grammar</td><td>Position of adjectives</td></tr>
<tr><td>Pronunciation</td><td>Silent consonants</td></tr>
<tr><td>Spelling</td><td>Words which are often confused</td></tr>
<tr><td colspan="2">14.2 Learn something new!</td></tr>
<tr><td>Vocabulary</td><td>School subjects</td></tr>
<tr><td>Exam skills</td><td>Listening Part 4: Gap-fill
Reading Part 3: Functional language</td></tr>
<tr><td>Grammar extra</td><td>*I prefer / I'd like*</td></tr>
<tr><td colspan="2">Preparation</td></tr>
</table>

Make a copy of the *When do you say this?* game board on the Teacher's Audio CD/CD-ROM (Photocopiable activities, page 11) for each pair of students. This will be used for the Extension activity in 14.2. Each pair will also need a dice.

14.1 Something good to read

SB pages 86–87

Reading

1 Ask students to work in pairs to do the questionnaire. As a round-up to this activity find out who reads most in the class and find out what type of book is the most popular.

Extension activity

Ask the class to prepare a paragraph about a book/story/magazine they like. They should write notes and then come to class prepared to persuade a small group of students to read their favourite story.

2 *Key* Reading Part 4

Ask the students to read through the three texts carefully. Check that they understand all the vocabulary. They should then look at the questions and decide on the correct answer. When they have finished they should compare their answers with a partner and talk about why they have decided on that answer.

Answers
1 C 2 B 3 A 4 A 5 C 6 A 7 B

3 Quickly elicit students' opinions on the books mentioned in the three texts.

Grammar

4 Refer students to the information about the order of adjectives before a noun. It is important that they realise that there is a pre-determined order, but at their level of English the main thing to remember is that opinion comes before fact.

Ask students to complete the chart with the underlined words in the photo story.

1 What's it like?	2 How big?	3 How old?	4 What colour?	5 Where's it from?	6 What kind?	NOUN
opinion	*size*	*age*		*nationality*		
	deep		blue			lake
good-looking				Australian		guitar player
great		new			computer	games

5 Students should use the chart to check the order.

Answers
1 a boring old book
2 a colourful new magazine
3 a modern Japanese computer
4 the excellent new school library
5 the long adventure book
6 the expensive little leather bag
7 a beautiful white dress
8 a clever young writer

6 In pairs, students should make sentences about the topics given.

Possible answers
1 I am reading a great new thriller. It is about this brilliant American scientist who finds a way of making people invisible.
2 My favourite item of clothing is a short, blue cotton skirt which I wear to parties.
3 My best friend is a fifteen-year-old French girl. She's tall and slim and I think she's very pretty.
4 My favourite film is the last *Harry Potter*. It's a really fast, exciting film.
5 I like Justin Bieber because he sings such brilliant, new songs.

Pronunciation

7 **2 11**

Answers
The silent letters are underlined.
1 li**g**ht
2 **k**nows
3 **gu**itar
4 w**h**at
5 w**h**o
6 of**t**en

8 **2 12** Students fill in the blank with the missing silent letter. They should practise saying the words in pairs. When they have finished, play the recording so they can check the pronunciation.

Recording script and answers
1 is**l**and
2 cas**t**le
3 hal**f**
4 clim**b**
5 autum**n**
6 kni**f**e
7 We**d**nesday
8 **h**our

Spelling sp**o**t

9 Students often confuse these words in the Writing part of the exam. Ask them to work through the exercise. They may have to make changes to the base word.

Answers
1 *Then* Suzy ran into the sea, but it was colder *than* it looked.
2 The weather was really *bad* when I was on holiday.
3 You don't *want* to stay in *bed* all day, do you?
4 She said, 'Bye' and went out to *buy* a book.
5 We are going to get some *things* from town.
6 I *won't* be home late tonight.

14.2 Learn something new!
SB pages 88–89

Vocabulary

1 Ask the class to work in pairs, putting the school subjects in the order they like them and using some of the *Key speaking* expressions to describe them.

2 Students discuss what subjects they would like to do, using the illustrations as a prompt.

Listening

3 Key Listening Part 4

2 13 Students are going to hear a conversation between a girl, Sylvia, and a man who works at a theatre school. They should listen and fill in the missing information.

Answers
1 November
2 (£)240
3 9.15 / a quarter past nine / nine fifteen
4 Marylebone (High Street)
5 189

Recording script
Man: Hello. Can I help you?
Sylvia: Yes, please. I'd like some information about Saturday classes at the school.
Man: I'm afraid the classes are full until the end of October. The new classes begin on 3rd November. Which classes are you interested in?
Sylvia: Singing and dance.
Man: OK. Can you send me a cheque and I'll keep a place for you? It's £120 for each class, so that'll be £240 then.
Sylvia: And what time do the classes begin? I'm free all morning.
Man: The school opens at nine o'clock on Saturdays and classes start at nine fifteen.
Sylvia: Could I visit the school to see what it's like?
Man: Of course. We're in Marylebone High Street – that's M-A-R-Y-L-E-B-O-N-E.
Sylvia: Thanks. Can I get a bus? I prefer buses to the underground.
Man: Yes, there's the 139 or the 189. The 189 stops right outside the school.
Sylvia: That's great. When can I come and visit?
Man: Any time. What about next week?
Sylvia: OK, I'll do that. Thank you very much.
Man: You're welcome. Goodbye.
Sylvia: Goodbye.

Reading

4 Key Reading Part 3

2 13 Ask the class to match sentences 1–4 with responses A–D. Play the recording again so they can check their answers.

Answers
1 C 2 D 3 B 4 A

5   **2** **14** Students should work in pairs to do this exercise. Then play the recording so they can check their answers.

Answers
1 G   2 E   3 I   4 H   5 F   6 J   7 A   8 D   9 C   10 B

Recording script

1
Girl: I can't come on the school trip.
Woman: What a pity.

2
Boy: What are you doing?
Girl: Chemistry homework.

3
Girl: I've got an exam tomorrow.
Man: Good luck!

4
Boy: I've passed all my exams.
Girl: Congratulations!

5
Woman: Would you mind opening the classroom window?
Boy: Sure, I can do that.

6
Girl: Where's the library?
Man: On the first floor.

7
Boy: Hi! How are you?
Girl: Fine, thanks.

8
Man: Is that your teacher?
Girl: No, it's not.

9
Man: Can I sit here?
Woman: I'm afraid it's taken.

10
Boy: Let's study together tonight.
Girl: Sorry, I can't – I'm going swimming.

Extension activity ◎

Each pair of students should have a copy of the *When do you say this?* game board on the Teacher's Audio CD/CD-ROM and a dice. When they land on a square with a speech bubble, they should say when/where this phrase is said. If they land on a blank square, they should wait for their next turn. The first person to the Finish is the winner.
If a student gets the answer wrong, they miss a go.

Possible answers
3   When it's someone's birthday.
6   You've won a prize, got married, passed an exam.
8   You've lost something, can't go to a party, etc.
9   When someone thanks you or says they are sorry.
11   In a shop, when you don't want to buy something.

12   Something bad has happened. You've spilt something, lost something.
13   On the phone, to say who you are.
14   When someone has said *thank you* to you.
17   At meal times, to refuse more food.
18   When you meet someone for the first time. They say *How do you do?* and you say *How do you do?*
20   When you are saying goodbye.
21   When someone has a headache.
22   When something doesn't matter.
24   When someone is looking for you.
25   When you agree with someone.
26   When you didn't hear what someone said.
27   When you didn't hear what someone said, or you want to attract someone's attention or you want to pass them.
28   In a shop.
29   When you see someone you know, or you know they've been ill.

6   Check that the class understands *Across* and *Down*. The answers are to do with learning.

Answers

Across		*Down*	
3	language	1	pen
4	library	2	study
6	board	5	bookshelf
7	listen	8	desk
9	teacher	10	cupboard
11	history	12	saw
13	homework		

Grammar extra

7   Ask the class to read the example sentence and complete the questions individually. Then they should ask and answer the questions with a partner.

Answers
2   Would you like to marry someone famous or someone who isn't famous?
3   Do you prefer eating in restaurants or going on a picnic?
4   Would you like to meet Angelina Jolie and Brad Pitt?
5   On your next holiday would you like to go to New York or Malibu Beach?
6   Do you prefer getting up early or staying in bed?
7   Where would you like to live?

Activity

Students should do this activity in small groups. At the end they need to give a short talk to the class. They could use drawings if they wanted to.

Exam folder 8

Reading Part 3 Multiple choice

SB pages 90–91

Ask students to read the information about this part of the Reading and Writing paper. Refer them also to the Exam advice and the example answer sheet.

Go through the example with them before they do the Part 3 task. Explain why the answer is B and why the other answers are wrong. Explain that it's normal to answer with 'it's' rather than 'I'm' in English on the phone. They should avoid just choosing A because the word 'Sally' is mentioned.

Now, ask the students to do Questions 11–15 and then 16–20.

Part 3

Answers

11	C	16	D
12	B	17	A
13	A	18	H
14	B	19	C
15	A	20	F

15 The world of work

15.1 Working hours	
Vocabulary	Jobs
Exam skills	Reading Part 4: Multiple choice – one long article
	Writing Part 6: Spelling
Grammar	Present perfect
Spelling	Words ending in -er and -or

15.2 Part-time jobs	
Grammar extra	*just* and *yet*
Exam skills	Listening Part 3: Multiple choice
Pronunciation	/ð/ and /θ/

Preparation

Make five copies of the *Good and bad points* grid on the Teacher's Audio CD/CD-ROM (Photocopiable activities, page 12) and write the name of a job in the first column of each row. This will be used in the Extension activity in 15.1. Make a copy of the recording script on the Teacher's Audio CD/CD-ROM (Photocopiable activities page 13) for each student. This will be used in 15.2.

15.1 Working hours
SB pages 92–93

Vocabulary

1 Ask students to match the jobs to the photos. The chef is Jamie Oliver.

Answers
1 nurse
2 photographer
3 chef
4 actor
5 farmer

2 Ask students what verb form is used in the definitions (third person singular present simple). Remind them that most verbs in the third person singular need an -s ending, like these. The omission of -s is a common error in the Key exam.

Answers
1 dentist
2 receptionist
3 tour guide
4 engineer
5 journalist

3 As a follow-up, ask students what job they would like to do in the future. Give them some time to think about their answers and then elicit ideas, giving help with vocabulary where necessary.

Extension activity ⊙

Make five copies of the *Good and bad points* grid on the Teacher's Audio CD/CD-ROM and write the name of a job in the first column of each row. Divide the class into five groups and give each group one of the grids. Ask the groups to write down the positive and negative points about each job. Then ask each group to report their ideas to the class.

Reading

4 **Key** Reading Part 4

Tell students to use the colour coding to help them locate the answers to the questions in the text. Give them up to ten minutes to decide on their answers. Then go through the questions with them and explain any answers that they have found difficult.

Point out the use of possessive forms and apostrophes in question 5 (*Jamie's wife; a friend of Jamie's wife*).

Answers
1 B   2 A   3 A   4 B   5 C   6 A   7 C

Grammar

5 Concentrate on form rather than use here.

Answer
The present perfect is formed with *has/have* and the past participle.

6 Ask students to match the two uses of the present perfect (A and B) to the four examples (sentences 1–4). Then point out the common error with *ago* and ask students to decide on sentences 5–7.

Answers
1 B   2 A   3 A   4 B
You must use the past simple with *ago* because it refers to a completed action in definite past time.
5 A
6 incorrect
7 A

7   Ask students to work through the exercise and then compare answers. Elicit which sentences are incorrect and write the corrected tenses on the board, together with the time phrases (underlined below).

Answers
Sentences **3**, **5** and **7** are incorrect:
3 The supermarket *advertised* for more staff <u>last week</u>.
5 Marion *became* a doctor <u>in 2011</u>.
7 Lee *arrived* for his meeting <u>an hour ago</u>.

8   Ask students to complete the text in pairs. Elicit answers and then ask students about the text. Would they like to live and go to school in another country? How would they feel if their parents travelled a long way every day for work, like Tom Stone?

Answers
2   moved
3   have made
4   has travelled
5   began
6   decided
7   meant / has meant
8   wasn't
9   found
10 has taken

9   Ask students to quickly tick the things they have done and then elicit answers to the question *Have you ever been to London?* round the class. If someone says *Yes*, add a second question, for example *When was that? What did you do?* Then tell students to ask and answer in pairs, using the list and adding a suitable second question. Walk round and check which tenses they are using (present perfect for the first question, past simple for the second).

Spelling spot

10 This is also useful practice for Writing Part 6. Ask students to read the information before they do the exercise. This can be set as homework if necessary.

Answers
1   photographer
2   painter
3   journalist
4   actor
5   doctor
The job in the yellow box is 'pilot'.

15.2 Part-time jobs
SB pages 94–95

1   Explain that in Britain many teenagers do newspaper delivery rounds, either before or after school, or do part-time jobs in the evening or at weekends. Elicit students' views on part-time jobs.

The photos show a girl delivering newspapers, a boy helping at a stable and a girl working in a cake shop.

2   Ask students to read the advertisements and then elicit answers.

Answers
1 B   **2** A   **3** C

3   Elicit students' views on voluntary work (advertisement C).

Ask students to read the information.
The *Cambridge Learner Corpus* shows that accurate use of *just* at *Key* (A2 level) is an indicator of above-average ability.

4   Ask students to write out the sentences in full. If time is short, ask students in pairs to write alternate sentences.

Answers
1   The receptionist at the sports centre has just left a message for you.
2   Tom hasn't met his new boss yet.
3   They haven't sent me any information about the job yet.
4   Nick's dad has just stopped working at the hospital.
5   My uncle has just given me a job in his café.
6   Charlotte and Andy haven't found a photographer for their wedding yet.
7   I have just chosen a computer course to go on.
8   The supermarket manager hasn't paid Mike for his extra hours yet.

Listening

5   **Key Listening Part 3**

   2 15 Give students exactly 20 seconds to read the questions and then play the recording twice.

Answers
1 B   **2** C   **3** B   **4** A   **5** B

Recording script

Sam: Melody Music Shop?

Kate: Yes, this is Kate Richards. How can I help?

Sam: My name's Sam Bennett. I've just seen your advertisement for a Saturday job. What are the hours?

Kate: The shop's open from ten to six but I need someone to <u>start at nine and stay until seven</u>. I'm always here from eight till eight on Saturdays so I really need some help then!

Sam: I see. What kind of help?

Kate: Well, the most important thing is <u>helping customers, being a shop assistant</u>. I also want someone to do a bit of cleaning at the end of the day, so I can do the money.

Sam: Fine. How much do you pay?

Kate: If you aren't 18 yet, it's £ 5.25 an hour.

Sam: Actually, I am 18.

Kate: Then it's <u>£6.30</u>, and after nine months I'll pay £7.00 an hour.

Sam: Sounds great! Er … where is the shop? I've never been there!

Kate: It's not in the town centre. If you know <u>the university, it's about three minutes' walk from there</u>.

Sam: I live in Weston, but I can cycle along the river to get there.

Kate: That's true. Well, any other questions?

Sam: When can I come and see you about the job? I'm free on Wednesday afternoon.

Kate: Sorry, I've got a meeting then. Um, how about Thursday or Friday?

Sam: <u>I can come early on Thursday</u>, at nine?

Kate: Fine. See you then.

Sam: Great!

Ⓟhotocopiable recording script activity ◎

Hand out copies of the recording script on the Teacher's Audio CD/CD-ROM (Photocopiable activities, page 13), where some words and phrases have been blanked out. Ask students to fill in as many as they can by looking again at the questions. Then play the recording, asking them to check their answers and add any missing words or phrases.

Answers

1 hours
2 most important thing
3 yet
4 three minutes' walk
5 free

Pronunciation

6 **2 16** The focus is on the sounds /ð/ as in *clothes* and /θ/ as in *thirsty*. Draw students' attention to the pictures. Play the recording and elicit the two sounds in the examples given: /ð/ and /θ/. Ask students to repeat the sentences.

2 17 Ask students to repeat the words they hear and write them in group 1 or group 2. Play the recording twice if necessary.

Answers

group 1 /ð/	group 2 /θ/
than	thunder
those	theatre
leather	thirty
	month
	nothing

Recording script

leather   month   nothing   than   theatre   thirty   those   thunder

---

7 **2 18** Explain that students should concentrate on the /ð/ sound (for example, *clothes*) the first time they listen and the /θ/ sound (for example, *thirsty*) the second time.

Answers

1 I've worked for <u>the</u> last two mon<u>th</u>s in my fa<u>th</u>er's shop.
2 Let's look at all <u>these</u> job adverts toge<u>th</u>er.
3 I <u>th</u>ought you were working at <u>the</u> museum. Have you finished <u>there</u>?
4 Jenny, <u>th</u>anks for looking <u>th</u>rough my article.
5 <u>That</u> footballer earns a hundred and <u>th</u>irty <u>th</u>ousand euros a mon<u>th</u>!
6 My bro<u>th</u>er's just got a job in the nor<u>th</u> of Sweden.

Activity

Write these places on the board: *department store, hospital, hotel, film studio*. Ask students to brainstorm different jobs at each place. The group with the most jobs at the end wins. (Check that all the jobs are plausible for the place!)

Possible answers

Place	department store
Jobs	manager, shop assistant, cleaner, driver
Place	hospital
Jobs	doctor, nurse, ambulance driver, cleaner
Place	hotel
Jobs	receptionist, cook, waiter, secretary, cleaner, engineer
Place	film studio
Jobs	actor, cameraman, director, make-up person, (script)writer

Writing folder 4

SB pages 96–97

Writing Part 8
Information transfer

Ask students to read the information about this part of the Reading and Writing paper. Explain that all the information that is needed in the answers appears on the question paper. In Part 8, candidates often lose marks unnecessarily by mis-copying a word or number.

1   Ask students to identify the kinds of text, which are typical of those used in *Key* Writing Part 8.

Answers
1   ticket
2   poster
3   email

2   Ask students to find the information and then compare answers.

Answers
1   07765 912448
2   *Animal Farm*
3   August 29 / 29.08
4   Juan Romero
5   £12.30
6   8.00 (pm) / 20.00
7   Brenton College (gardens)
8   £5.75

Part 8

Ask students to do the exam task, following the Exam advice given.

Answers
51   lauratou@free.fr
52   18
53   23 June / June 23 / 23.06
54   Eastbourne
55   (£)60

16 Transport

16.1 Journeys	
Vocabulary	Transport (nouns and verbs)
Grammar	Modal verbs 2: *should*, *must/mustn't*, *need to/needn't*, *don't have to*

16.2 A day out	
Vocabulary	Free-time activities
Exam skills	Speaking Part 2
	Listening Part 1: Multiple choice
Pronunciation	Weak and strong forms
Spelling	*i* or *e*?

16.1 Journeys
SB pages 98–99

1 Ask students to read the sentences (1–4) and decide in pairs whether they are true or false.

Answers
1 False – The world's largest airport in land area is King Fahd International Airport in Dammam, Saudi Arabia, at 790 sq km.
2 True
3 True
4 Partly false – It was a sheep, a duck and a chicken!

Vocabulary

2 Ask students to sort the transport words, writing the correct words alongside. Elicit answers.

Answers
1 train
2 coach
3 bicycle
4 boat
5 plane
6 motorbike
7 helicopter
8 horse

3 Ask students to match these words to their pictures and elicit any more words.

Answers
a 7 b 1 c 8 d 6 e 2 f 3 g 4 h 5

4 Elicit possible verb–noun collocations. Remind students to list new vocabulary like this where appropriate.

Answers
catch – a coach, a train, a plane
drive – a train, a coach
fly – a plane, a helicopter
get – a coach, a train, a plane, a helicopter, a boat
get off/on – a train, a coach, a bicycle, a boat, a plane, a helicopter, a horse
park – a coach, a motorbike
ride – a bicycle, a motorbike, a horse
sail – a boat
take off – a plane, a helicopter

Grammar

5 Elicit the difference between examples 1 and 2, reminding students of the meaning of *must* if necessary. Then discuss the difference between sentences 3 and 4.

Answers
1–2 *Should* gives advice here (and the girl doesn't have to act on it); *must* holds an obligation – it is essential that this girl is at Gate 43 by six o'clock or she won't be allowed to board the plane.
3–4 *Mustn't* is a prohibition (i.e. you must go earlier than six o'clock); *don't have to* means it isn't necessary to go there before six o'clock, but you can if you want to.

6 Suggest students complete the text on their own and then compare answers. Point out that they can use each verb once only.

Answers
1 should
2 don't have to
3 must
4 mustn't

7 Ask students to decide in pairs which modal verbs are the closest in meaning to *need to* and *needn't* here. Explain that there is no *to* after *needn't* (*needn't to* is a common error at this level).

Answers
1 *need to* – The closest verb is *must*.
2 *needn't* – The closest verb is *don't have to*.

8 Ask students to choose the correct modal verb in the sentences. If time is short, this exercise can be done for homework.

9 Ask students to look at the example and describe the journey from London to Vizzavona. Elicit answers and then encourage students to describe another journey using as many transport words as they can. They could of course 'invent' a really complicated journey!

Possible answer
You need to fly to Paris first. You should change planes there and fly to Ajaccio. You needn't hire a car at the airport. You should take a taxi to the station. Then you can take a train to Vizzavona.

16.2 A day out
SB pages 100–101

Vocabulary

1 Elicit students' ideas for the three different days out. They can use some of this language in the Speaking Part 2 tasks (exercises 4 and 5).

Possible answer
Visiting a big city – go shopping, go sightseeing, take photos of old buildings
Hiking in the countryside – walk around a lake, look for wild animals, go swimming in a river
Spending a day at the beach – play volleyball, go fishing, go surfing

2 Ask students to match the verbs to the nouns in pairs. Some of these phrases will be useful in exercises 4 and 5.

Answers
build a sandcastle
climb a hill
fly a kite
have a picnic
kick a football
throw a Frisbee
visit a museum

Speaking

3 **Key Speaking Part 2**

Remind students that the Speaking test is in two parts. Ask them to decide in pairs whether the sentences are right or wrong. Elicit answers with reasons.

Answers
1 Right – Each candidate has a turn at asking the five questions.
2 Wrong – You must base your answers on the information given on the card.
3 Right – You should talk only to the other candidate.
4 Wrong – You should use some other words and expressions, to make the conversation sound as natural as possible and to show your language range.
5 Right!

4 Ask students to decide in pairs who will be Student A. Then ask students to turn to the relevant page and give them enough time to complete the task (about two minutes per turn).

5 Students stay in the same pairs and this time Student B asks the questions and A answers.

Extension activity

Offer to record each pair as they do a practice Speaking test, setting up individual times for this. Give them the recording so that they can note down their own errors, and suggest areas for improvement.

Listening

6 **Key Listening Part 1**

2 19 Explain that students will hear each conversation twice. Play the recording and then elicit answers.

Answers
1 B 2 B 3 C 4 B 5 A

Recording script
1 *Which train is leaving first?*
Man: Excuse me, is this the Bristol train?
Woman: No, this one's leaving for Oxford in five minutes. There's been a change to the Bristol train. You need to go over the bridge to platform 4.
Man: Oh dear, have I got enough time to get there?
Woman: Plenty, that's the London train that's ready to leave now. Yours will be the next train after that one.
Now listen again.
(The recording is repeated.)
2 *How will the girl get to the cinema?*
Girl: Can you tell me where the ABC cinema is, please?
Man: Certainly. Turn left at the next traffic lights and then take the second on the right.
Girl: Is that Green Street?
Man: That's the turning after. It's Robertson Road you need. Go nearly to the end and you'll see the cinema on your left.

Now listen again.
(The recording is repeated.)

3 *Where is Kate's boat now?*

Adam: Hi, Kate! We've just sailed past that little island. How far have you got?

Kate: Well, Adam, I can't describe anything because there's <u>water all around</u>. We went under a bridge about a quarter of an hour ago, if that means anything?

Adam: Sounds like you'll get to our meeting place in about an hour, then.

Kate: Sorry it's taking so long. Bye.

Now listen again.
(The recording is repeated.)

4 *How will the woman get to work today?*

Anne: Mike, it's Anne. Listen, there are no trains this morning because of last night's winds. <u>Is it OK if I get a taxi</u> in to work? Will the company pay?

Mike: Can't you use your car? It's much cheaper.

Anne: I'm afraid it's at the garage.

Mike: <u>OK, then,</u> but make sure you ask for a receipt. See you later.

Now listen again.
(The recording is repeated.)

5 *Where is the nearest petrol station?*

Woman: Can you tell me where I can get some petrol?

Man: Well, the cheapest place is on the motorway. It's not far. You can get on at the next roundabout.

Woman: I really need a nearer one. I haven't got much left.

Man: I see. Turn left by the lights, then, and you'll find one on the right <u>next to a bank,</u> about 200 metres down that road.

Now listen again.
(The recording is repeated.)

Pronunciation

7   **2 20** Ask students to listen carefully to the examples. If necessary, play the recording again so that students recognise the weak forms.

2 21 Then play the next track and ask them to decide about sentences 1–8, writing W or S. Check answers, playing the recording again and pausing so that they can hear each one.

Answers
2 W   3 S   4 W   5 W   6 W   7 S   8 W

8   These examples of errors are taken from the *Cambridge Learner Corpus.*

Answers
1 museum
2 airport
3 hospital
4 (correct)
5 university

Activity

Ask students to take it in turns to give directions. Walk round listening as they do the activity and summarise any recurring errors on the board afterwards.

Units 13–16 Revision

SB pages 102–103

This revision unit recycles the language and topics from Units 13–16, as well as providing exam practice for Reading Part 5 and Writing Part 7.

Speaking

1 Ask students to draft their questions and then ask and answer in pairs.

Possible questions
2 Shall we go swimming at the beach later?
3 Do you want to go for a pizza after class?
4 What does your favourite jacket look like?
5 What's the weather going to be like at the weekend?
6 How much does it cost to get into the club?
7 Have you visited any other countries?
8 Have you read any good books recently?

Grammar

2

Answers
The correct sentences are:
1 B 2 A 3 C 4 B

3

Answers
1 C 2 B 3 B 4 A 5 C 6 B 7 A 8 C

Vocabulary

4 Ask students to do this in pairs.

Answers
Jobs
Nouns: actor, chef, dentist, farmer, journalist, photographer, receptionist, tour guide
Verbs: build, grow, phone, write
Weather
Nouns: cloud, fog, rain, snow, storm, wind
Verbs: rain, snow
Transport
Nouns: boat, car, helicopter, motorbike, plane
Verbs: catch, drive, fly, get off, park, sail, take off

5

Answers
1 C 2 B 3 B 4 A 5 A 6 B 7 B 8 C

Writing

6

Answers
1 any
2 one/magazine
3 ago
4 lots/plenty
5 every/each/this/next
6 most
7 something
8 by
9 were
10 never

17 Science and technology

Preparation

Make a copy of the recording script on the Teacher's Audio CD/CD-ROM (Photocopiable activities, page 14) for each student. This will be used in 17.2.

17.1 Totally Techno
SB pages 104–105

Reading

1 Ask students to do the quiz to find out what their attitude to science and technology is. When they have finished ask them to compare answers with a partner. Do they agree with their results?

Grammar

2 Make sure students understand what an infinitive of purpose is. Then ask them to look back through the quiz and find the four infinitives of purpose. (Not all the infinitives with *to* are infinitives of purpose.) For more practice, refer students to the Grammar folder.

Answers
You use your computer <u>to play</u> games until late every night.
You don't like using Facebook <u>to chat</u> to friends.
You hate using the computer <u>to do</u> your homework.
You could use it <u>to help</u> your social life

3 This exercise gives more practice in the use of infinitives of purpose. Check the vocabulary is familiar and then ask students to work through it.

Answers
2 to download
3 to turn on
4 to call
5 to keep
6 to listen
7 to study
8 to buy

4 Ask students to work through this exercise in pairs. They should think of as many reasons as possible why people do these things.

Possible answers
2 People use Google to search for information.
3 People buy electric cars to be green.
4 People go to other countries to learn a language and to find out about different cultures.
5 People play computer games to have fun.
6 People use a laptop computer to work outside or to work on the train.
7 People read magazines to find out about one of their interests.
8 People play team sports to get fit / have fun / keep healthy.
9 People learn English to get a good job or to travel.
10 People buy the latest technology to be cool.

5 Take a few minutes to have a class discussion about life with no electricity.

Ask the students to look at the *Did you know?* boxes. Check they understand the contents.

Ask them to read the email and web addresses and check they can pronounce them correctly. Ask some students to tell you their own email address and some web addresses they know.

6 *Key* Reading Part 5

Ask the class to read through the text about a girl who had to spend some time with little or no access to modern technology, such as the internet. It is important that students really understand the text before they start to do the exam task. It is a very bad idea to go straight to the multiple-choice questions without reading the text first.

Answers
1 A 2 C 3 A 4 B 5 B 6 A 7 C 8 B

17.2 New ideas
SB pages 106–107

1 Check the class understand the definition of a gadget. Ask the students to look at the pictures of various gadgets. They should talk about which gadgets they like and say why they find them interesting.

Listening

2 | Key | Listening Part 3

2 22 This listening task is about a gadget exhibition in London. Ask the students to read through the questions first to get an idea of what they will hear. Then play the recording twice.

Answers
1 C   2 A   3 B   4 C   5 C

Recording script
Edward: Hi, Vanessa! Did you have a good weekend?
Vanessa: Great! I had a fun weekend. I went to see a special gadget show in London.
Edward: Sounds interesting, but I think shows like that are too expensive – I paid £15 last time I went.
Vanessa: This was only £9.50. I did buy a guidebook as well – that was an extra £5.95.
Edward: How did you get there?
Vanessa: You can take the underground, but I got the bus. It stops just outside. I got very tired walking around all day, though.
Edward: What did you see?
Vanessa: Well, the Games Hall was my favourite, but there was an interesting 3D Theatre and also a large Test Space.
Edward: It sounds great! How early can you go in? At nine?
Vanessa: You can't go in until ten, and we didn't get there until eleven thirty, so there wasn't enough time to see everything.
Edward: Can you eat there?
Vanessa: Yes. You can even take a picnic! I had a sandwich at a café but you can get a hot meal at the restaurant.
Edward: I'd really like to go. I'm free next Saturday – that's 23rd April.
Vanessa: The show's only on until the 27th, so the Saturday may be busy.
Edward: Well, I'll go on the 24th, then.

Photocopiable recording script activity ⊙

Download copies of the recording script from the Teacher's Audio CD/CD-ROM and hand them out after the first listening. Play the recording again and ask students to locate the answers. Make them aware of the distractors.

Pronunciation

3   **2 23**

Answers
You *cannot* go in until ten.
We *did not* get there until eleven thirty.
There *was not* enough time to see everything.
I *would* really like to go.
I *am* free next Saturday – *that is* 23rd April.
I *will* go on the 24th.

4   **2 24** Students should work through this exercise, forming contractions. There are two sentences where contractions can't be formed. Play the recording so students can check their answers.

Recording script and answers
1 I'm going to buy a new calculator.
2 Aren't you coming to my house tonight?
3 Who's playing with my PlayStation?
4 I'd like a new phone for my birthday.
5 (can't be contracted)
6 Dan's borrowed my laptop again.
7 They can't get any batteries because the shop's closed.
8 (can't be contracted)

Vocabulary

5 Collocations were introduced in Unit 5. This unit covers *get*, *give*, *have*, *make*, *see* and *watch*.

Answers
get   a job; a bus
give   a party; someone a call
have   a party; a good time; a job; friends
make   friends; a noise; a film
see   a film; friends
watch   a film; TV
We normally say *watch TV* and *see a film*, though *watch a film* is sometimes also possible.

6

Answers
1 make   2 get   3 make   4 watch   5 see   6 given
7 give

7   This can be done in class or at home. It contains typical errors made by *Key* candidates.

Answers
Hi everyone
I want to sell my phone *because* my girlfriend *bought* me a new *one* last *weekend. It* is *two months* old. *The price* was about $100 and *I'm selling* it for $50. *Does anyone* want to *buy* it?

Extension activity

For homework ask students to write a For Sale notice for a computer game, computer or other item that they own. They should include details of:
• how much it originally cost
• the sale price
• details of the product.

Explain the use of the infinitive with and without *to*. It may be useful at this point to revise the *-ing* form of verbs, which was covered in Unit 11, as students sometimes wrongly use an *-ing* form instead of the infinitive.

8   Students can work through this exercise in pairs or individually. These are typical *Key* candidate errors.

Answers
1   I'd like *to see* you next weekend.
2   I must *arrive* home at 10.00.
3   I would like *to sell* my books.
4   I want *to buy* it.
5   You can *go* to a museum there.
6   I have decided *to study* chemistry.
7   She should *visit* London.
8   I hope *to see* you soon.
9   We need *to do* our homework tonight.
10 We went to London *to see* the London Eye.

Activity

This activity recycles vocabulary learnt in Unit 10 – materials. Ask the class to guess what the object described is. (Answer – a mobile phone.)

Ask them, either in class or for homework, to write a short description of an everyday object. The rest of the class must guess what it is.

Exam folder 9

SB pages 108–109

Listening Part 3
Multiple choice

Ask students to read the information about this part of the Listening paper. Also make sure they fully understand the Exam advice.

Before the exam task, go through the two examples of exam-type questions and make students aware of the use of distractors in the exam. They should realise that they will often hear more than one of the three options mentioned on the recording and that they have to process the information to get the right answer. (The answer to Example 2 is C.)

Part 3

2 25

Answers
11 B   12 A   13 C   14 C   15 A

Recording script

Listen to Ellie talking to Chris about Lynne, his sister. For questions 11 to 15, tick A, B, or C. You will hear the conversation twice. Look at questions 11 to 15 now. You have 20 seconds.

Ellie: Hi, Chris. I hear Lynne's here. I thought she was coming on Saturday.

Chris: Yeah, well, <u>she came on Wednesday</u> because she has to be at work again on Monday.

Ellie: That's a pity. How is Lynne's new job with that computer company?

Chris: Great. She did a course in London and <u>now she's in New York</u> for a year. Next year she may go to Hong Kong!

Ellie: That's brilliant! I'd like to work with computers.

Chris: Me too, but Lynne didn't study anything to do with computers at school. Dad <u>taught her at home</u> and then she did maths at university.

Ellie: She must work hard.

Chris: Yes, but she gets four weeks' holiday a year. <u>Next year it'll be six</u> – my dad only gets five!

Ellie: Can I see her tomorrow?

Chris: Of course. Come <u>in the afternoon</u>. She'll be in bed all morning.

Ellie: OK, I'll come after lunch. I've bought her a watch for her birthday.

Chris: Wow, Ellie, she'll love that! She really wanted me to get her a camera but I only had enough money <u>for a computer game, so I got that</u>!

Ellie: I'm sure she'll like it. See you tomorrow.

Now listen again.

(The recording is repeated.)

---

18 Health and well-being

<table>
<tr><td colspan="2">18.1 Keeping well!</td></tr>
<tr><td>Vocabulary</td><td>Parts of the body</td></tr>
<tr><td>Exam skills</td><td>Reading Part 6: Spelling
Reading Part 3: Functional English
Listening Part 5: Gap-fill</td></tr>
<tr><td>Grammar extra</td><td>Word order of time phrases</td></tr>
<tr><td>Pronunciation</td><td>Linking sounds</td></tr>
<tr><td colspan="2">18.2 A long and happy life</td></tr>
<tr><td>Exam skills</td><td>Reading Part 4: Right, Wrong, Doesn't say
Writing Part 9: Writing a note</td></tr>
<tr><td>Grammar</td><td>First conditional</td></tr>
<tr><td>Spelling</td><td>Words which don't double their last letter, as in *helped*, *needed*</td></tr>
<tr><td colspan="2">**Preparation**</td></tr>
<tr><td colspan="2">Make one copy of the *How stressed are you?* board game on the Teacher's Audio CD/CD-ROM (Photocopiable activities, page 15) for each group of four students. This will be used in the Extension activity in 18.2. Each group will also need a dice.</td></tr>
</table>

18.1 Keeping well!

SB pages 110–111

Vocabulary

1   Ask the class to correctly spell the parts of the body 1–12 and then to match them with the pictures.

Answers

1	head d	5	hands j	9	ear c
2	hair b	6	back l	10	mouth i
3	neck k	7	leg a	11	nose e
4	arm f	8	foot h	12	eye g

2   *Key* Reading Part 6

The task is about words connected with health. Students must decide what the word is and spell it correctly.

Answers

1 sick   2 nurse   3 ambulance   4 medicine
5 temperature   6 chemist

Extension activity

Ask students to do the same as the above by writing six definitions of other words to do with health, the body and fitness. They must then get their partner to guess the words.

3   *Key* Reading Part 3

The section deals with responses to common medical complaints. Students should work in pairs to match the complaint to the response. There may be more than one appropriate response, depending on nationality.

Suggested answers

1 H   2 J   3 E   4 B   5 C   6 F   7 I   8 A   9 G   10 D

4   Ask students to work in pairs and look at the pictures. They should take it in turns to say what is wrong with them and to give advice.

Possible answers

1   I think I've broken my leg.
   – Why don't you go to hospital? / You should call an ambulance.
2   I've got stomach ache.
   – Why don't you lie down?
3   I've got toothache.
   – You need to see a dentist.
4   I've cut my knee.
   – You should put a plaster on it.
5   I've got a cold.
   – You need to drink some hot lemon juice and go to bed.
6   I've got a headache.
   – Why don't you take an aspirin?

Listening

5   *Key* Listening Part 5

2 26 Tell the class that they are going to hear a recorded message giving information about chemists which are open in the local area. Give them time to read through the questions and then play the recording.

Answers

1   6.30 (p.m.)
2   Peters
3   17
4   (the) cinema
5   01921 6582

Recording script

Thank you for calling for information about the opening hours for chemists in your area. This information is for the week of the 15th to the 21st December. There are two chemists, one in Sandford and one in Dursley. Bridges Chemist in Sandford opens at eight forty-five from Monday to Saturday and closes at <u>six thirty p.m.</u> Monday to Friday and at twelve thirty p.m. on Saturday. The shop is at 53 Green Street, Sandford. There is a small car park next to the shop.

Outside those hours, please go to Peters. That's <u>P-E-T-E-R-S</u>. This is in Dursley at number <u>17</u> The High Street. It's on the other side of the road to <u>the cinema</u> and is open from ten thirty a.m. to four thirty p.m. on Sundays and has late opening to eight p.m. on weekdays. The telephone number is <u>01921 6582</u>. Ring this number if you need to talk to the chemist at night. You can park in the High Street on Sundays.

Grammar extra

Refer the class to the information in their books.

6   Students should work through the exercise. It is more usual to place the time phrase at the end of the sentence, although it depends on which part of the sentence you wish to emphasise – the time or the action. Where it is possible to place it at the beginning of the sentence, this is shown in brackets.

Answers
1   (Last night) I was at a big party last night.
2   (On Saturday) I'll come shopping on Saturday.
3   We have been to the beach every day.
4   (After work) I went to the chemist after work.
5   They usually sleep well at night.
6   (Today) I bought some new trainers today.

Pronunciation

7   **2** 27

Recording script and answers
1   Can‿you call‿an‿ambulance?
2   Fruit‿and vegetables‿are very good for you.
3   You should do some‿exercise‿every day.
4   Watching TV‿all weekend‿is not good for you.
5   Make sure you get‿enough sleep‿at night.

18.2 A long and happy life
SB pages 112–113

Speaking

1   Tell the students to ask three others about their sleeping habits. They should work through the questions and fill in the questionnaire so that they will have the information to report back to the class.

Reading

2   **Key** Reading Part 4

Ask the class to read the article quickly to find out who is the oldest person mentioned (Shirali Muslimov). Students should then read the article again and answer the questions.

Answers
1 A   2 B   3 C   4 B   5 C   6 A   7 A   8 B

Grammar

Ask the class to find the sentence in the text which begins with If ...

Answers
If you eat a little but often, you will live a long life.
The tenses used are:
If + eat (present simple), + will live (future simple)

3   For more practice, refer students to the Grammar folder on page 147 of the Student's Book.

Suggested answers
1 E   2 D   3 A   4 F   5 B   6 C

Extension activity ◎

Make a copy of the How stressed are you? board game on the Teacher's Audio CD/CD-ROM (Photocopiable activities, page 15) for each group of four students. They will need a dice to play. The questions should not be taken too seriously.

4   The class can work in pairs or groups to do this discussion on health. Ask them to talk about the ideas mentioned and to add two ideas of their own.

5 Ask students to work in pairs and discuss the type of problems they may have on a camping holiday, and how they will solve them. Problems could be:

you run out of food/money/water
you lose your way
it rains every day
you lose your bag
your tent leaks
you get bored

6 The class should write down four sentences which are true for them. They should all begin with *If*.

7 Key Writing Part 9

This can be done in class or set for homework.

Sample answer
Dear Tina,

I want to get fit so I can climb a mountain with my father in the summer. I am going to go running every day and I will do this from tomorrow morning!

Love,

Julia

This answer includes all the key points and is error-free. It would receive full marks.

8 Check students understand the explanation and ask them to complete the exercise.

Answers
1 ✓
2 ✗ – faster
3 ✓
4 ✗ – stopping
5 ✓
6 ✓
7 ✗ – thinner
8 ✗ – swimming

Activity

This activity is for homework and then the information found can be reported back the next day. The students should prepare a chart and write out the question prompts 1–5 in full in class. They then take their chart home and find the oldest person they know to interview and write down the replies on their chart.

Exam folder 10

SB pages 114–117

Reading Part 4 Multiple choice

In Part 4 of the Reading and Writing paper students may get either one long article with multiple-choice questions or three short articles with multiple-choice questions. For both types of text, there are seven questions with an example at the beginning, and each question has a choice of three answers (A, B or C).

One long article

1 Refer the students to the Exam advice. They should then look at 1. Explain that there are distractors in the text. Students will find it helpful to underline the part of the text which contains the answer.

Answer
1 C

2 Ask the students to do the exam task.

Answers
21 B   22 C   23 B   24 A   25 C   26 A   27 B

Three short articles

Refer students to the Exam advice.

Answers
21 C   22 A   23 B   24 A   25 B   26 C   27 B

19.1 Let's communicate!

Vocabulary	Communicating
Exam skills	Listening Part 2: Multiple matching
	Writing part 7: Open cloze
Pronunciation	Stressed syllables
Grammar	Prepositions of place
Spelling	Spellings of the sound /iː/

19.2 Different languages

Exam skills	Reading Part 5: Multiple-choice cloze
Grammar	Prepositions of time
Vocabulary	Countries, languages, nationalities

Preparation

Make a copy of the recording script on the Teacher's Audio CD/ CD-ROM (Photocopiable activities, page 16) for each student. This will be used in 19.1.

19.1 Let's communicate!
SB pages 118–119

Vocabulary

1 Suggest students spend a couple of minutes finding the words on their own and then compare the words in pairs. Elicit answers and check understanding if necessary, using the pictures.

> **Answers**
> *Across*
> call envelope facebook text message
> write telephone
> *Down*
> internet send email receive mobile postcard
> ring note

2 Ask students to discuss in pairs for about five minutes. Then elicit ideas.

Listening

3 **Key** Listening Part 2

2 28 Remind students that in this matching task the example letter (B) cannot be used again, so there are seven choices for five questions. Play the recording twice before eliciting answers.

> **Answers**
> 1 D 2 F 3 A 4 E 5 G

> **Recording script**
> **Paul:** Hello, Ruby.
> **Ruby:** Hi, Paul. I've just seen your Facebook page. Congratulations on getting the job!
> **Paul:** Thanks. Mario's travelling up to Scotland today so he hasn't been online this morning. I spoke to him on his <u>mobile</u> instead.
> **Ruby:** Good. Have you told <u>Anna</u> yet?
> **Paul:** Well, I left a <u>message</u> on her <u>phone</u>, but I think she's away. If I don't hear from her, I'll send her a text tomorrow.
> **Ruby:** And what about your brother, <u>Jack</u>? He's away too, isn't he?
> **Paul:** Yes, in Argentina. I <u>emailed</u> him from home this morning after I opened the letter about the job. I know he'll be pleased.
> **Ruby:** Was <u>Tessa</u> still in the flat when the post arrived?
> **Paul:** No, but I've left a <u>big note</u> on the kitchen table for her.

Ruby: Remember to phone <u>your professor</u> and tell him.

Paul: I can't, because the number at the university has changed. Anyway, I've already told him the news on a <u>postcard</u>. I bought one of that Moroccan carpet we saw at the museum.

Ruby: He'll like that.

Photocopiable recording script activity ◉

Make copies of the recording script from the Teacher's Audio CD/CD-ROM and hand them out. Several verbs in verb–noun collocations are blanked out. Ask students to add each verb in the correct tense, using the nouns to help them remember the verb. Then play the recording again so that they can check their answers.

Answers
1 seen 2 spoke 3 left 4 send 5 opened 6 arrived
7 changed 8 told

Pronunciation

4 **2 29** Play the recording and ask students to place a star or dot above the stressed syllable of each word. Play it again for them to check their answers and repeat the sentences after the recording.

Suggest students mark the stress on new words they write down, particularly when they are of three or more syllables.

Answers
2 Mario's trá|vel|ling up to Scót|land to|dáy.
3 I spoke to him on his mó|bile in|stéad.
4 I left a méss|age on her phone.
5 Yes, in Ar|gen|tí|na.
6 Re|mém|ber to phone your pro|féss|or and tell him.
7 The núm|ber at the u|ni|vér|si|ty has changed.
8 I bought one of that Mo|rócc|an cár|pet we saw at the mu|sé|um.

Grammar

Explain that candidates often make mistakes with prepositions. This lesson focuses on prepositions of place and 19.2 looks at prepositions of time.

5 Give students two minutes to do the exercise and then elicit answers, writing some of their examples on the board.

Answers
2 on 3 in 4 in/on 5 at 6 in 7 at

---

6 Ask students to correct the sentences in pairs. Elicit answers.

Answers
1 You can call me *on* my cell phone: 22 59 67 81.
2 I'll meet you *at/in* the supermarket in West Street.
3 I'm *on* holiday now in Istanbul.
4 You can stay *at/in* my house.
5 The hotel is *in* the centre of the town.
6 We live *in* a new house in Magka.
7 (correct)
8 If you are interested in joining the club, find me *in* room 12.

7 This exam-level task can be set for homework if time is short.

Answers
1 many 2 because/as/since 3 some 4 on
5 In 6 these 7 Which 8 will 9 me
10 everyone/everybody

Spelling spot ◉

8 Ask students to study the examples and add the missing vowels. Dictionaries can be used to check spellings if necessary.

Answers
1 received 2 free; each 3 speak 4 field
5 week 6 kilo

Extension activity

Organise the class into groups of three or six. Explain that you are going to have a competition to produce as many words with the same spelling of /iː/ as possible. Write the three words *see*, *mean*, and *believe* on the board and underline their /iː/ spellings, as in the Spelling spot lists.

Give students up to ten minutes to write down more words with the same spelling (in beginning, middle or end positions). They could take one spelling each (group of three) or per pair (group of six), and then add to each other's lists. If students are struggling to think of words, suggest they look through the Vocabulary folder on pages 149–152, or give them one dictionary per group. Note that the *-ie-* spelling is less frequent than the other two, so students may not come up with as many words. The group with the highest number of correctly spelled words wins.

Possible answers
1 seen, been, feet, bee, sleep, green, referee, free, cheese, tree, week
2 read, ice cream, tea, eat, dream, pleased, cheap, jeans, clean, team, teacher, colleague, easy, speak, speaker, each, beach, peace, reach
3 believed, field, niece, piece, achieve, brief, chief, thief

19.2 Different languages

SB pages 120–121

1 Elicit answers from students and talk about your own use of dialects or other languages.

2 Ask students to answer the quiz on their own and then compare answers.

Answers

1 *Wrong* – Spanish is spoken by about 390 million people, but Mandarin Chinese is spoken by more than 1000 million people (845 million native speakers, 1025 million total – figures from 2000).

2 *Wrong* – Japanese is not an official language of the UN. The six languages are: English, French, Spanish, Russian, Arabic, Chinese.

3 *Right* – More than 700 living languages are spoken in Indonesia. Most belong to the Austronesian language family, with a few Papuan languages also spoken. The official language is Indonesian (locally known as *Bahasa Indonesia*), a modified version of Malay, which is used in commerce, administration, education and the media, but most Indonesians speak local languages, such as Javanese, as their first language. Many Indonesians living in urban areas are also taught English as a second language beginning at the elementary school level.

4 *Right* – There are many '*bilinguals*' who do not use *standard* Italian as their main language, and some say they may account for nearly half the population in Italy (source: Wikipedia).

5 *Wrong* – The text in exercise 3 explains this in more detail.

Reading

3 [Key] Reading Part 5

Ask students to read the article and then decide on the answers.

Answers

1 C 2 B 3 C 4 B 5 A 6 C 7 B 8 C

Grammar

4 Ask students to complete the explanation with the correct prepositions.

Answers

We use *in* with years, etc.
We use *on* with days, etc.
We use *at* with times, etc.

5 Ask students to work in pairs and get Student Bs to put up their hands. They should turn to page 135 and answer Student As' questions about Lara's timetable. Student As should fill in the timetable and, when they have finished, check it against the one on page 135.

6 Suggest students fill in the chart in pairs.

Answers

country	nationality	language(s) spoken
Argentina	Argentinian	Spanish
Brazil	Brazilian	Portuguese
Chile	Chilean	Spanish
France	French	French
Greece	Greek	Greek
Italy	Italian	Italian
Mexico	Mexican	Spanish
Morocco	Moroccan	Arabic, French
Switzerland	Swiss	French, German, Italian, Romansch

Activity

Divide the class into two teams and ask students in each team to number themselves from 15 onwards (this gives practice of the larger numbers). Say the numbers and ask students to put up their hands as their number is called. There should be two students with the same number, one on each team. If one team has an extra person, take that person's number yourself for the other team.

Call a number, for example 22. The person whose number it is in team A should say the name of a country. The team B person then has to name one language that is spoken there. The next time, the team B person says the name of a country and the team A person has to name a language. Keep alternating in this way.

Keep a record of points awarded on the board, in tally style (⊪⊪ = 5), and add up the points at the end to decide the winning team.

Here is a longer list of countries and languages, in case students need more help.

country	nationality	language(s) spoken
Algeria	Algerian	Arabic, French
Austria	Austrian	German
Belgium	Belgian	Flemish, French
China	Chinese	Chinese
Croatia	Croat	Croatian
Denmark	Danish	Danish
Egypt	Egyptian	Arabic
Eire (Ireland)	Irish	English, Irish, Gaelic
Finland	Finn	Finnish
Germany	German	German
Holland	Dutch	Dutch
Japan	Japanese	Japanese
Korea	Korean	Korean
Norway	Norwegian	Norwegian
Poland	Polish	Polish
Portugal	Portuguese	Portuguese
Russia	Russian	Russian
Slovenia	Slovenian	Slovene
Spain	Spanish	Spanish
Sweden	Swedish	Swedish
Turkey	Turkish	Turkish

Writing folder 5

SB pages 122–123

Writing Part 9 Short message

Ask students to read the information about this part of the Reading and Writing paper. There are two kinds of Part 9 task: 'with input' and 'instructions only'. Writing folder 3 covered the 'with input' type.

1 These Part 9 answers have been taken from the *Cambridge Learner Corpus*. Ask students to decide on the three points in the task, choosing from A–E.

Answers
A, C, D

2 Elicit views, asking students for their reasons why.

Answers (and marking information)
Answer 3 is the best and would score 5 marks. It has only one error (*in the bus stop*) and all parts of the message are clearly communicated.

Answer 2 is the worst and would score 1 mark. Only one piece of information is communicated and the answer is short (23 words).

Answer 1 would score 4 marks. It is just long enough at 25 words and contains some errors in spelling and grammar.

Answer 4 would score 3 marks. All three parts of the message are attempted but the reader needs to interpret some of the information. There are also some errors in grammar and spelling. Although there is no penalty for answers that are longer than 35 words, this message reads unclearly at 53 words. See improved version in 4 below.

3 Suggest students do this on their own and then compare answers.

Answers

1
Dear Pat
I'll be free at 10 a.m. We can meet us at Paul's caffe. I'd like to buy a skirt. See you on Saturday.
Love Anya

2
Dear Pat
I will go for two hours. I will meet with John and I will want to buy a red bicycle.
Your friend

3
Dear Pat
I think it is a great idea to go shopping together. We could meet at the bus stop at 12 o'clock in the morning. I'd like to buy some pens.
See you soon. Claudia

4
Yes, I coming with you to shopping on Saturday. I'll probably be free at the lunch. We'll meet us at the shopping centre in town. I want to buy me two trousers and a top. Perhaps, I want to buy also a robe. And you, what do you want to buy? From your best friend Sylvie

4 Explain why it is better for students to write according to the word limits given (see marking information in 2 above).

Improved answer
Dear Pat,

I'm free to go shopping at lunchtime on Saturday. Let's meet at the shopping centre in town. I want to buy two pairs of trousers, a top and perhaps a dress too.

From your best friend,

Sylvie

Part 9

Ask students to write their answers following the Exam advice given.

Sample answer
Hi Jan,

Let's meet at the cinema at 7.30 tomorrow. I really want to see *Hugo*. You'll love it because your favourite actor, Asa Butterfield, is in it. See you inside.

Love,

Kirsten
(33 words)

20.1 Famous people	
Grammar	Review of tenses
Exam skills	Reading Part 4: Multiple choice
20.2 Lucky people	
Exam skills	Listening Part 4: Gap-fill
	Speaking Part 2
	Writing Part 6: Vocabulary
	Reading Part 2: Multiple choice
Pronunciation	Sentence stress
Vocabulary	Describing people
Spelling	*ck* or *k*?
Preparation	

For the activity in 20.2, make copies of the 'money' on the Teacher's Audio CD/CD-ROM (Photocopiable activities, pages 17–18) and cut it into notes. You will need about 30 × 1000 KETO (pronounced *Keeto*) notes and 20 × 2000 notes. Add more 1000 notes for a large class.

20.1 Famous people

SB pages 124–125

1   Elicit who is shown in the pictures: left – the Spanish footballer Cesc Fabregas; centre – the British actor Emma Watson; right – the Colombian singer-songwriter Shakira. Lead a class discussion on the questions raised.

2   Elicit answers round the class.

3   Suggest students answer the questions in pairs.

Answers
1   B (Shakira was born in 1977 and Emma Watson in 1992)
2   C
3   A
4   C
5   B

Grammar

4   Ask students to do the exercise in pairs. Elicit answers, asking students to say which tense is used and why

Answers
1   has sold (present perfect with since)
2   became (past simple with definite time in the past)
3   won't play (negative future reference – Fabregas transferred to Barcelona in August 2011)
4   was growing up (past continuous for temporary situation in the past)
5   talks (present simple – habitual present)

5   Ask students to use a similar range of tenses in their sentences.

6   Suggest students compare their sentences and tick the tenses used.

Reading

7   *Key* Reading Part 4

Elicit what facts students already know about Emma Watson. Then give them ten minutes to answer the multiple-choice questions. Elicit answers and reactions to the article.

Answers
1 B   2 C   3 B   4 A   5 C   6 C   7 A

8   Ask students to find examples of the different tenses.

Answers
The present continuous isn't included in the article.

present simple:	doesn't want, enjoys, feels, understands, is, says, are
present continuous:	NONE
past simple:	wanted, was, didn't know, missed, had, got, meant, chose, earned, understood, mattered, kept
past continuous:	was learning, were filming
present perfect:	have been, hasn't given, have understood
future with *will*:	will never need

20.2 Lucky people

SB pages 126–127

1 Elicit students' ideas. If necessary, give your own opinion first.

2 Ask students whether they know of any sports stars who do these strange things – for example, Rafael Nadal puts his drinks bottles down in a certain way. Elicit students' ideas as to why he does this.

Possible answer
Sports stars do this to bring them luck.

3 Suggest that students work through the chart in pairs.

4 Ask students to discuss where they will go and who they will take. Elicit answers round the class.

Listening

5 **Key** Listening Part 4

2 30 Play the recording twice and then elicit answers. Check spellings of 1, 3 and 4 and remind students that in 3, *Saturday* must have a capital letter.

Answers
1 train/rail 2 30(th) 3 Leyton 4 Saturday 5 11.15

Recording script
Ruth: Hello, this is Ruth Barnes. I've just heard I've won this month's radio competition!
Man: Ah yes. Congratulations.
Ruth: Thanks. What have I won?
Man: You're lucky, it's two return tickets to <u>Venice</u> from anywhere in Britain.
Ruth: I'll go with my mum. But is that by plane? She doesn't really like flying.
Man: No problem, they're <u>train tickets</u>.
Ruth: Great! When do we have to use them by?
Man: Well, you must travel before <u>30th</u> April, but today's only April 5th, so there's plenty of time.
Ruth: We can go during my school holidays. Will you send me the tickets?
Man: No, you must come to our office and sign for them.
Ruth: Where are you?
Man: The address is 47 <u>Leyton</u> Road. That's L-E-Y-T-O-N. It's near the theatre.
Ruth: When shall I come? I'll be at school tomorrow and Friday.
Man: <u>Saturday</u> morning, then. And you can have a look around the radio station if you'd like to.

Ruth: Great. What time? About ten thirty?
Man: Let's say <u>eleven fifteen</u>, then you can say hello to DJ Richard Rooster. His show finishes at eleven.
Ruth: I've always wanted to meet him. Thanks very much.
Man: No problem. We'll see you soon.

Pronunciation

6 **2 31** Ask students to underline one word only in each question. Play the recording.

Recording script and answers
1 What have I <u>won</u>?
2 When do we have to <u>use</u> them by?
3 Will you <u>send</u> me the tickets?
4 Where <u>are</u> you?
5 When shall I <u>come</u>?
6 What <u>time</u>?

Speaking

7 **Key** Speaking Part 2

Explain that students should try to put suitable stress on one word in each question as they do the Part 2 task. Give them up to three minutes to complete each task and walk round listening to them, so that you can summarise any common errors on the board afterwards.

Vocabulary

8 **Key** Writing Part 6

Ask students to fill in the missing letters for each word. Elicit answers.

Answers
1 special
2 kind
3 single
4 clever
5 happy
The adjective in the yellow squares is *angry*.

Reading

9 **Key** Reading Part 2

Check understanding of *millionaire*. Go through the exercise quickly, eliciting answers.

Answers
1 B   2 C   3 B   4 A   5 C   6 A

Spelling sp⊙t

Ask students to read the information before they do exercise 10.

10 This exercise can be set as homework if necessary.

Answers
1 clock   2 jacket   3 booking; tickets
4 lucky   5 chicken

Activity

Make copies of the 'money' on the photocopiable activity sheet on the Teacher's CD-ROM and cut it into notes. Make sure you have at least 30 x 1000 KETO (pronounced *Keeto*!) notes and 20 x 2000 notes (add more 1000 notes for a large class; see question 20 below). Award the money suggested in brackets for a correct answer; take one 1000 note back for each wrong answer.

Millionaire quiz

1 Spell the name Scarlett Johansson. (1000 for each part of name)
2 Spell the plural of *sandwich*. (1000)
3 What is the opposite of *always*? (1000)
4 What is the past tense of *buy*? Spell it. (1000 + 1000 for spelling)
5 Name an animal that is found in Africa. (3000)
6 Spell the word *easiest*. (1000)
7 Name four words for clothes you wear outside. (1000 per word + 5000 bonus if all four are correctly spelled)
8 What do you say instead of *must* in the past tense? (2000)
9 Give examples of two future tenses. (1000 per tense)
10 Name four things you can find in a bedroom. (1000 per word + 1000 bonus for four)
11 Spell the *-ing* form of the verb *swim*. (2000)
12 Who is your father's brother to you? (3000)
13 What is the weather like today? (1000 for an adjective; 4000 for a longer response)
14 Spell the word *enough*. (3000)
15 What is the present perfect tense of the verb *find*? (2000)
16 Name four things that can travel on a road. (1000 per word + 1000 bonus for four)
17 Why do we have fridges? (up to 6000 according to the quality of the response)
18 Name four parts of the body. (1000 per word + 1000 bonus for four)
19 What language is spoken in Brazil? (1000)
20 Who is the most famous footballer today? (see below)

Allow the whole class to have an opinion on the most famous footballer and award 1000 to anyone who answers the question with a name + 3000 for a longer response, reason, etc.

Extension activity

If students like the quiz, suggest they devise their own questions as a homework activity. Allocate a different unit in the course to each student and remind them to include questions on spelling as well as vocabulary and grammar.

Units 17–20 Revision

This revision unit recycles the language and topics from Units 17–20, as well as providing exam practice for Reading Part 2 and Writing Part 9.

Speaking

1 Encourage students to give long and detailed answers.

Grammar

2 Give students a couple of minutes to write their sentences. Elicit answers round the class.

Possible answers
1 If I buy a new phone, I'll be able to send photos.
2 If I get a Saturday job, I'll earn some money.
3 If I become famous, I'll build a house with a pool.
4 If I eat more healthily, I'll feel better.
5 If I have a party, I'll invite all my friends.
6 If I do all my homework, I'll go out with my friends.
7 If I go on the internet, I'll visit some new websites.
8 If I take a break soon, I'll get a cup of coffee.

3

Answers
Martinique is the largest island *in* the area of the eastern Caribbean. Over 300,000 people live *on* the island – many *in* the capital city, Fort-de-France. People speak French and it is taught *in/at* schools.

The mountains on Martinique are old volcanoes. The highest one is Mount Pelée, which is 1,397 metres high. *In* 1902, Mount Pelée erupted and about 30,000 people were killed.

The weather *in* Martinique is warm and quite wet – perfect for the farmers to grow bananas *on* their land. Bananas from Martinique are sent all over the world, so look at the bananas *in* your fruit bowl. If they are from Martinique, they will have a blue sticker *on* them.

Vocabulary

4 There may be more than one correct answer.

Suggested answers
1 robot (not to do with a computer)
2 back (not part of the face or head)
3 envelope (not a type of written communication)
4 Japanese (not European)
5 prize (the result, not what is done)
6 ready (not necessarily positive)

5

Answers
1 C 2 A 3 B 4 B 5 A

Writing

6 Ask students to match the sentences to A or B. They could rewrite the two answers for homework.

Answers
A 2, 5, 6
B 1, 3, 4

Answers to Grammar folder exercises

Unit 1

1A

2 Can your sister come tomorrow?
3 Are Carmen and Maria from Brazil?
4 Do you like dogs?
5 Is it time to go?
6 Does Arturo catch the same bus?

1B

2 How do you get to school?
3 Where is your house?
4 What have you got in your bag?
5 Why are you angry?
6 Who does Ingrid know?

Unit 2

2 any 3 any 4 some 5 some 6 any 7 some 8 any

Unit 3

3A

2 Does (Pete really) hate 3 love 4 doesn't eat 5 goes
6 Do (you usually) go 7 don't sell

3B

2 g 3 d 4 a 5 e 6 h 7 b 8 f

Unit 4

2 Did you enjoy 3 didn't arrive 4 made 5 travelled
6 did Lyn see 7 did Pete go 8 didn't speak
9 did she spend 10 did she buy

Unit 5

2 but 3 because 4 and (but would also be possible)
5 Because 6 or

Unit 6

2 less expensive 3 the tallest 4 richer 5 sunnier
6 The most popular 7 the fastest 8 more expensive
9 better 10 the worst

Unit 7

2 was trying on; lost 3 was waiting; remembered
4 was choosing; went off 5 was studying; began
6 phoned; was having; left

Unit 8

2 may/might 3 must 4 can't 5 had to 6 has to
7 may/might 8 can

Unit 9

2 are going to 3 will 4 am / 'm going to 5 will 6 will / 'll
7 is / 's going to 8 will 9 will 10 is / 's going to

Unit 10

2 Portuguese is spoken in Brazil.
3 The Pyramids were built by the Egyptians.
4 The *Harry Potter* books were written by J. K. Rowling.
5 Presents are given on birthdays.
6 Spaghetti is eaten all over the world.
7 I was taught to swim by my father.
8 Chocolate is sold in sweet shops.
9 The World Cup was won by Spain in 2010.
10 The car was stopped by the police.

Unit 11

2 swimming 3 choosing 4 using 5 sitting; watching
6 getting 7 running 8 riding

Unit 12

2 everything 3 Somebody/Someone 4 something
5 Everybody/Everyone 6 nobody / no one

Unit 13

2 too dry 3 too wet 4 hot enough 5 cold enough
6 too strong

Unit 14

2 a large wooden reading desk
3 a popular American music magazine
4 an interesting adventure story
5 a friendly young detective
6 my favourite French comic book

Unit 15

2 Joan has just taken the customer's order.
3 Giorgio has just become a doctor.
4 Someone has just left a message for you.
5 I've just seen our dentist crossing the street.
6 I've just spoken to the engineer on the phone.

Unit 16

2 and 5   3 and 8   4 and 7

Unit 17

2 I turned on the radio to listen to the news.
3 I went to the museum to see an exhibition.
4 I borrowed some money to buy a computer game.
5 I worked hard to pass the exam.
6 I bought a cake to take to the party.

Unit 18

2 If you eat an apple a day, you won't get ill.
3 If you don't eat too many sweets, you won't get fat.
4 You will / You'll lose weight if you stop eating snacks.
5 Your teeth will stay healthy if you visit the dentist once a year.
6 You will / You'll have bad dreams if you eat cheese in the evening.

Unit 19

19A

2 in   3 at   4 in   5 at   6 in/on   7 at   8 on   9 at   10 in

19B

2 on   3 at   4 in   5 on   6 in   7 at   8 in

Unit 20

2 has (just) made   3 is going out   4 ate
5 stopped; was driving   6 won   7 asks

Answers to Practice for Key Writing Part 6

Unit 1
1 free 2 happy 3 wrong 4 sick 5 funny

Unit 2
1 camera 2 toys 3 shampoo 4 umbrella 5 card

Unit 3
1 fruit 2 salad 3 cake 4 pasta 5 soup

Unit 4
1 arrive 2 return 3 carry 4 decide 5 visit

Unit 5
1 horse 2 cow 3 duck 4 elephant 5 chicken

Unit 6
1 expensive 2 modern 3 bright 4 closed 5 attractive

Unit 7
1 jacket 2 socks 3 pockets 4 trousers 5 sweater

Unit 8
1 drum 2 guitar 3 album 4 lights 5 piano

Unit 9
1 luggage 2 passport 3 guidebook 4 ticket 5 map

Unit 10
1 mirror 2 curtains 3 lamp 4 pillow 5 carpet

Unit 11
1 baseball 2 football 3 surfing 4 volleyball 5 tennis

Unit 12
1 parents 2 cousin 3 uncle 4 granddad 5 sister

Unit 13
1 wind 2 rain 3 snow 4 ice 5 storm

Unit 14
1 geography 2 maths 3 science 4 history 5 music

Unit 15
1 farmer 2 nurse 3 waiter 4 dentist 5 chef

Unit 16
1 plane 2 ship 3 train 4 coach 5 bicycle

Unit 17
1 videos 2 website 3 email 4 laptop 5 program

Unit 18
1 medicine 2 doctor 3 temperature 4 chemist
5 toothache

Unit 19
1 envelope 2 note 3 stamp 4 postcard 5 text

Unit 20
1 single 2 famous 3 kind 4 awesome 5 worried

Sample answer sheet – Reading and Writing (Sheet 1)

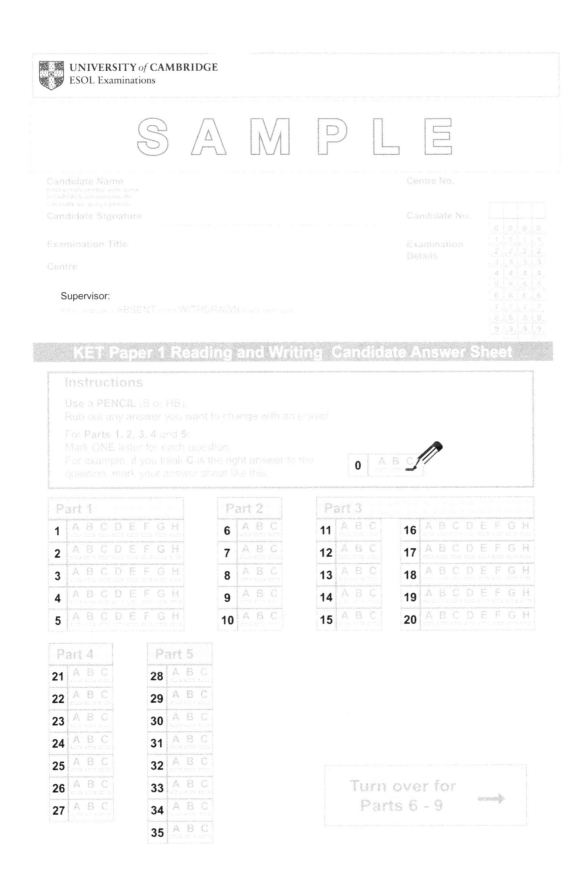

Sample answer sheet – Reading and Writing (Sheet 2)

For **Parts 6, 7 and 8:**

Write your answers in the spaces next to the numbers (36 to 55) like this:

0	example

Part 6		Do not write here
36		1 36 0
37		1 37 0
38		1 38 0
39		1 39 0
40		1 40 0

Part 7		Do not write here
41		1 41 0
42		1 42 0
43		1 43 0
44		1 44 0
45		1 45 0
46		1 46 0
47		1 47 0
48		1 48 0
49		1 49 0
50		1 50 0

Part 8		Do not write here
51		1 51 0
52		1 52 0
53		1 53 0
54		1 54 0
55		1 55 0

Part 9 (Question 56): Write your answer below.

Do not write below (Examiner use only)

0	1	2	3	4	5

Sample answer sheet – Listening

S A M P L E

Candidate Name
If not already printed, write name
in CAPITALS and complete the
Candidate No. grid (in pencil)

Centre No.

Candidate Signature

Candidate No.

Examination Title

Examination
Details

Centre

Supervisor:

If the candidate is ABSENT or has WITHDRAWN shade here

KET Paper 2 Listening Candidate Answer Sheet

Instructions

Use a PENCIL (B or HB).

Rub out any answer you want to change with an eraser

For Parts 1, 2 and 3:
Mark ONE letter for each question.
For example, if you think C is the right answer to the
question, mark your answer sheet like this.

0   A B C

Part 1		Part 2		Part 3	
1	A B C	6	A B C D E F G H	11	A B C
2	A B C	7	A B C D E F G H	12	A B C
3	A B C	8	A B C D E F G H	13	A B C
4	A B C	9	A B C D E F G H	14	A B C
5	A B C	10	A B C D E F G H	15	A B C

For Parts 4 and 5:
Write your answers in the spaces next to the
numbers (16 to 25) like this.

0   example

Part 4		Do not write here		Part 5		Do not write here
16		1 16 0		21		1 21 0
17		1 17 0		22		1 22 0
18		1 18 0		23		1 23 0
19		1 19 0		24		1 24 0
20		1 20 0		25		1 25 0

The **Objective Key Second Edition Teacher's Resources Audio CD / CD-ROM** can be used in both your CD player and in your computer. Use it in your CD player to listen to the Practice Test audio tracks. Use it in your computer to also view the Practice Test, Progress Tests, Wordlists and other PDF resources.

Using this disc on your computer
The software can be run directly from the disc and does not require installation.

System Requirements
- Windows XP, Vista or 7
- Mac OS X 10.5, 10.6 or 10.7
- 1024 x 768 minimum screen resolution
- Speakers or headphones
- PDF reader

To run the disc:
Insert it into your CD-ROM drive.

Windows
- If **Autorun** is enabled on your computer, the software will start automatically.
- If **Autorun** is not enabled, open **My Computer**, right-click the **CD-ROM drive**, and then choose **Explore**. Double click the file **ObjectiveKeyTeacher.exe**.

Mac
- Double-click the **Objective Key Teacher CD-ROM** icon on your desktop to open it.
- Double-click the **Objective Key Teacher** icon.

Using this disc in your CD player
The disc contains recordings for the Practice Test Paper 4 which you can listen to on your CD player.

Technical support
For support and updates, go to www.cambridge.org/elt/support

Terms and conditions of use